PROVERBS

Nihon Ki-in's Handbook Series

Vol. 1: *Proverbs*

Master the fundamentals with this book, which explains over 150 traditional sayings for improving your go, organized by subject and illustrated with hundreds of informative diagrams.

Vol. 2: *Fuseki*

This systematic outline of common openings examines twenty-nine basic strategies and explains the ideas behind standard moves so you can take advantage when your opponent refuses to follow the flow of the game.

Vol. 3: *Joseki, Part 1*

The third volume in the series covers corner play based on the 3–4, 4–5, and 4–6 points and includes refutations for many non-joseki moves.

Vol. 4: *Joseki, Part 2* (in preparation)

This volume covers corner play based on the 4–4 and 3–3 points, including double approach moves, and explains the balance of territory against influence in the opening.

Vol. 5: *Handicap Go* (planned)

The last book in the series explains how to use your handicap stones to best advantage, illustrating the basics of handicap go through discussion of games ranging from nine stones down to three.

PROVERBS

TRADITIONAL WISDOM
FOR
THE GAME OF GO

TRANSLATED AND EDITED
BY MAX GOLEM

YUTOPIAN ENTERPRISES
SANTA MONICA, CALIFORNIA USA

ISBN 1 - 889554 - 24 - 3 (Proverbs Handbook)
ISBN 1 - 889554 - 23 - 5 (The Handbook Series)

Originally published in Japanese by the Nihon Kiin as

Kakugen Kojiten, in the Shin-Hayawakari Series.

Layout Assistance - Craig Hutchinson
Proof Assistance - Paul Adams, Anthony Blagrove, Robert Meyer, Jeff Newmiller, Barry Phease and Chris Touzeau.

...for understanding *proverbs* and parables,
the sayings and riddles of the wise.
The fear of the Lord is the beginning of knowledge,
but fools despise wisdom and discipline.

Proverbs 1:6,7 NIV

Yutopian Enterprises
2255 29th Street, Suite 3
Santa Monica, CA 90405 USA
1-800-988-6463
Email: yutopian@netcom.com
Web Page: http://www.webwind.com/go
Coming soon, http://www.yutopian.com

1 2 3 4 5 6 7 8 9 10

ABRIDGED CONTENTS

Introduction

The Early Game

The Stones Go Walking

COMPLETE CONTENTS

Chapter 1. Basic Moves and Concepts

Chapter 2. Good Shape and Bad

Chapter 3. Playing Ko

Chapter 4. The Opening

play at the fulcrum between two moyos.

Chapter 5. Joseki
don't get boxed into the comer,

Chapter 6. Territorial Frameworks

Chapter 7. Life and Death

Chapter 8. Running, Connecting, and Capturing

Chapter 9. Clever Moves, Forcing Moves, and Sacrifices

Chapter 10. A Guide to Fighting

Chapter 11. A Potpourri of Proverbs

PREFACE

The game of go has been popular in the orient for centuries and, over the years, a great many proverbs have arisen to help players remember various aspects of the game. For example, there are sayings pertaining to the life and death of groups and to a variety of fighting techniques. Some proverbs help remind players how to play certain josekis, and others provide advice about one's general approach to the game, philosophy, and fighting spirit.

A study of this book will prove rewarding to all players. A beginner, confused by the many possible moves at every turn, will find what have become standard responses to common moves and much guidance in general situations. Stronger players will appreciate specific instruction in middle-game fighting and strategy.

This book can be used to look up proverbs that one may have heard but perhaps not fully understood, to study systematically for a knowledge of fundamentals that is hard to locate in other go books, or just to dip into from time to time on a casual basis.

We hope you will enjoy this collection of traditional go wisdom and that you will send any comments or suggestions to Yutopian Enterprises.

PART I

INTRODUCTION

Chapter 1
Basic Moves and Concepts

Gote no sente.

An understanding of the concepts of sente and gote is vital to playing go above the beginner level. A move is said to be sente if it is big enough to require an immediate answer. (Note that you should not make a move just because it is sente – forcing your opponent to strengthen his group or eliminate bad aji is the mark of a beginner.) A move is gote if your opponent can afford to ignore it and play somewhere else.

"Gote no sente" is a Japanese phrase that refers to a move that is gote but whose follow up is sente. The gote-no-sente technique, properly applied, will improve your game scores considerably.

Don't play go if you can't read a ladder. Capture a ladder as soon as you can.

Figure 1. The basic ladder is shown to the right, and is one of the first fighting techniques one learns in go. It takes some practice to read ladders accurately but, since they usually have no variations, everyone is capable of mastering them fairly quickly – it just takes a bit of effort.

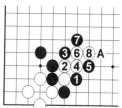

Figure 1. The ladder.

You should always capture a stone caught in a ladder as soon as possible, before your opponent has a chance to make a valuable play that the ladder will run into. If your opponent can force you to take the stone caught in the ladder by playing another move in another part of the board, he can often gain a significant advantage there. Such a move can be very efficient and is called a ladder breaker.

Ladders are one of the most common techniques in go – even if there is not an outright capture by ladder, there is at least the threat to do so in every game. You can't really play go if you do not understand ladders.

Each move in a failed ladder costs seven points.

Obviously trying to run away in a ladder that doesn't work is bad, but suppose you want to try pulling out the stones in the ladder as a series of ko threats? How much do you lose anyway? Modern analysis seems to agree that every time you extend a losing ladder, you take a loss of nearly seven points.

This is about two-thirds of a handicap stone for *each* move. For example, if you needed three dead-ladder threats to win a ko fight, you would have given up about twenty-one points. That means the ko had better be worth a good bit more. An interesting ko fight will probably entail at least seven ko threats on each side. If you pulled out a ladder to give you these threats, the ko would have to be worth forty-nine points just to break even!

And it is even worse – while the other person continues to atari your ladder stones, he is placing potential ladder breakers across the board, which may affect any other ladders that may arise.

You're best off by never pulling out a failed ladder for any reason. You also want to capture your ladder at the earliest opportunity.

There are no ladders in a nine-stone game. A ladder is six spaces wide.

This proverb is a comment on how effective a large number of handicap stones on the board can be. White, for the most part, has to avoid variations that require a favorable ladder, and this very much restricts what he can do.

A ladder is four stones across, but an enemy stone on either side will break it, so a ladder's field of operations is six spaces wide – more than the five-space separation between the star points. This is one reason why white tries to negate black's influence quickly in a high-handicap game.

The one-point jump is never bad.

You will hear this proverb often from strong players when you admit to having no idea where to go next. It is very good advice – even though a one-point jump may be a little slack in a given position, it is rarely bad.

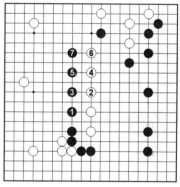

Figure 2. This position is from a professional game. Black makes one-point jumps all the way across the board, and white has no choice but to try to stay ahead. Black chases white because he can turn the potential balance of territory around to his

Figure 2. The one-point jump is powerful.

advantage without hurting his own position . The result is rather one-sided – black has destroyed white's prospects for a large territorial framework while the white stones haven't accomplished much.

Figure 3. This position is from a five-stone game. Black 4 and 8, marching out to connect to the center star point, are magnificent moves that give black a strong, thick position. Black 4 in particular is a powerful move that puts considerable pressure on the two isolated white stones. Playing elsewhere and allowing white to cap the marked black stone with 5 at 4 would enlarge white's field of operations and allow him to introduce complications. Ignoring the corner for the moment showed excellent judgement.

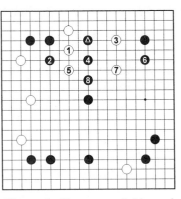

Figure 3. The one-point jump in a five-stone game.

Figure 4. The last example is from a nine-stone game. Black 8 and 14, connecting to the center star point, separate the white groups and give black a great position while white has played passively and is in great trouble.

The one-point jump is a move that you should get in the habit of playing and will come to appreciate as you become stronger. Be patient and, when in doubt, jump out into the center.

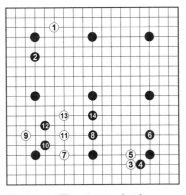

Figure 4. The one-point jump in a nine-stone game.

The two-point jump is quick but can be cut.

The two-space jump moves out into the center more quickly than the one-space jump, but it is much weaker. The two-space jump can be the perfect move for the situation, but you have to be ready with countermeasures in case your opponent decides to cut it.

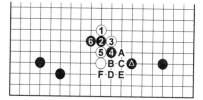

Figure 5. Cutting the two-space jump.

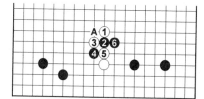

Figure 6. Cutting the other way.

Figure 5. Black 2 starts the cut immediately, and 4 is a skillful continuation. White pretty much has to atari with 5 and, after 6, he has the sequence **A** through **F** to weaken the marked black stone – this compensation is more than adequate for white.

Figure 6. Playing on the other side with white 3 is also possible, but this has the danger of becoming an overplay because of the cut at A. (White 3, curling around an enemy stone, is called a hane.)

The kosumi is never bad.

The diagonal move, or kosumi (really a hane without the enemy stone) can be a little slow, but it is rarely bad. It is fully connected to its base stone and quite strong. In many situations, a kosumi is the perfect move to make.

Connections: tight, hanging, and knight's.

There are various ways to connect stones, but the moves shown in the next three figures are the most common.

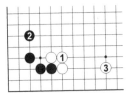

Figure 7. The tight connection.

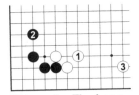

Figure 8. The hanging connection.

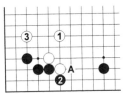

Figure 9. And the knight's connection

Figure 7. The tight, or solid, connection is less popular than it once was, but it is still seen quite often. It can't be cut and is immune to a peep.

Figure 8. The hanging, or loose, connection is a bit more popular because it allows you to play one space farther with 3, but there are a couple of peeps that the opponent can play which compensate for this advantage.

Figure 9. The knight's connection is a special move most often seen when black has a stone as shown at the star point just above it or one point to the left of either. This connection is rather loose – black could cut with 2 instead, but this would be bad because white will just force black up and to the left with one atari after another, gaining considerable outside thickness. If black plays at **A** after the basic sequence, white should extend four or five spaces up the left side.

Extend two spaces from a single stone.
Extend three spaces from a two-stone wall.
Extend four spaces from a three-stone wall.

These proverbs give the farthest safe extensions on the third line. There are exceptions in actual play, but these positions can be invaded and you must have a countermeasure in mind when you exceed these limits (such as attaching to the invader to build thickness or attaching to a nearby stone to make your wall higher before attacking the invader).

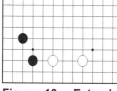

Figure 10. Extend two from one.

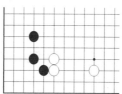

Figure 11. Extend three from two.

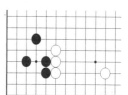

Figure 12. Extend four from three.

Figures 10, 11, and 12. These are the basic extensions that everybody should know. Although black can harass these groups with a capping play, shoulder hit, or "submarine" attack, the stones cannot be separated unless white is careless. Note that there is no proverb for extending five spaces from a four-stone wall – there's just too much room for complications in this case to generalize.

The two-space extension is secure.

Extending two spaces from a single stone on the third line forms a relatively safe, stable group (Figure 10 shows an example). As long as you respond to any attack, it should live without too much trouble.

The two-space extension is a bit slow and not often made unless the opponent approaches first; however, it is a good way to edge closer to a thick position cautiously.

Use the shoulder hit against the two-space group.

Because of its stability, the two-space group is often used as a base on which to frame a moyo. In this case, the shoulder hit is an ideal reducing move.

Figure 13. The shoulder hit of 1 is ideal for reducing the white framework here. After this sequence, the white group at the bottom is a little congested – white would rather have the marked stone one space farther away ("Extend three from two").

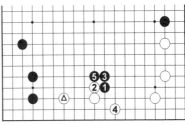

Figure 13. Ideal reducing move.

Instead of the shoulder hit, black could try the capping play at 5 or attaching to the right of the marked stone, though these moves are not as effective as the shoulder hit here.

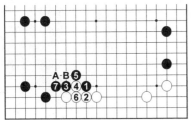

Figure 14. A strike on the other side.

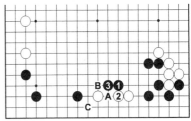

Figure 15. Another good shoulder hit.

Figure 14. In this figure, it is black who has the territorial framework (or moyo) and wants to enlarge it. The shoulder hit of 1 is again the best move, but played from the other side this time. Black builds thickness with 3 through 7. This is a more efficient result than if black had started with **A**. At times, white can answer 1 by jumping with **B** but allowing black to block at 2 would be severe here.

Figure 15. Here's another application of the shoulder hit. White will probably answer 1 with 2, then black must play 3 to prevent white from swelling out there and making good shape.

Black may be able to push through at **A** and cut, depending on white's answer. If white plays next at **B**, black **C** is an effective sente move. As long as white's stones are under attack, he has to postpone any plans to invade the lower side.

Answer the side attachment by extending.

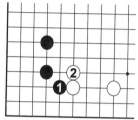

Figure 16. Extend!

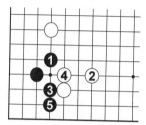

Figure 17. Here, too.

Figure 16. Black often attaches in this position to make white overconcentrated (according to the proverb, "Extend three spaces from a two-stone wall," the white stone to the right should be one space farther away for the most efficient shape). The attachment also strengthens black's corner somewhat, though it doesn't prevent a 3–3 invasion.

White has to extend to 2 even though it makes his stones a bit heavy. This move reduces the effectiveness of any attack black may launch here, and maintains some sort of contact with the center. If white plays somewhere else, just imagine how good a follow up at 2 would be for black.

Figure 17. Black 1 stops an easy white connection and threatens to press between 2 and 4 with a knight's move. Black 3 keeps white from sliding into the corner to make a base for his stones (and thus deprive black of one). Then white 4 prevents black from making perfect shape and black drops to 5 to complete the corner sequence, or joseki.

Keep an eye on bad aji.

Aji, literally "taste," refers to any lingering potential in a position. This potential is not often utilized immediately – for instance, the choice between a peep or a cut is sometimes better put off until later in the game when the local situation has become more settled, or an invasion may be delayed until a move can be played to reduce the thickness that the opponent will build up in response to the invasion.

A fine example of aji is that hoshi, the star point, is open to the 3-3 invasion. Being on the fourth line, the hoshi's strength lies in its influence toward the center; it is much weaker in making territory than a stone on the third line. It follows, then, that you should try to develop a hoshi stone by making wide extensions (preferably to other hoshi) to reinforce its central influence.

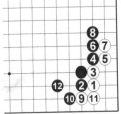

Figure 18. Weakness of the star point.

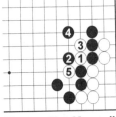

Figure 19. More aji to be watched.

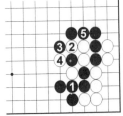

Figure 20. The continuation.

Figure 18. White will usually make an approach move first, but this is what happens if he invades at the 3–3 point right away. White's ten points or so of territory are worth far less than the outside influence that black gets, so white usually plays an approach move before invading.

Figures 19 and 20. If white cuts at 1 immediately to take advantage of the weak point in black's formation (another example of aji), black will follow the sequence in these two diagrams but it all comes to naught when black plays atari on the three white stones in Figure 20.

Instead, white will wait until a fight in this area adds a helpful stone to bring this aji back to life. Black has to remain aware of this possibility when conducting operations in this part of the board.

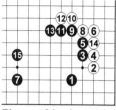

Figure 21. Leaving a joseki with bad aji.

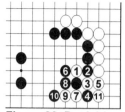

Figure 22. Punishing black.

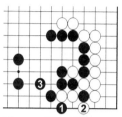

Figure 23. The correct way to end it.

Figure 21. Let's consider one last example. This figure shows the first fourteen moves of a joseki that is sometimes seen when black is thick in the lower left corner. White 14 is a powerful move: it protects against the black push at 14 and cut to the right of 6. It also introduces aji into the black position by reducing the number of liberties of moves 3 and 5. Black should have played 15 at hoshi to fix his shape, but the greedy jump seemed bigger.

Figure 22. White will play immediately as shown here to take advantage of black's lapse in judgement.

Figure 23. Black finishes up with 1 and 3 here. Black 3 is necessary, as white will play at the center of three stones then cut to the right of 3 if black neglects to protect against it. (Ignoring aji can really hurt you!)

Strike at the waist of the keima.

The keima, or knight's move, is great for chasing an enemy group and sliding into corners but, away from the side of the board, it can be cut. The keima's weakness is its "waist," which consists of the two intersections between the two stones.

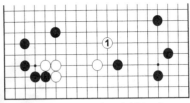

Figure 24. How should black answer?

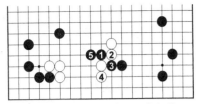

Figure 25. Play at the waist, then cut.

Figure 24. White has played 1, perhaps thinking to reduce the black framework on the right and get some breathing space for his nearly encircled stones at the same time, but trying to do too much has gotten him into trouble. How should you punish white?

Figure 25. Black 1 is just the move. After the exchange shown, white is in for a real fight. Note that first pushing at 2 then cutting above 1 is not very good for black.

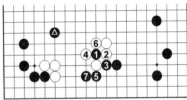

Figure 26. If the marked stone were not there, this would be almost playable.

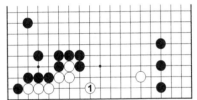

Figure 27. Another example: it is black's turn to play.

Figure 26. White's biggest mistake was allowing himself to get boxed in like this in the first place.

For the sake of argument, imagine that the marked black stone has not been played. In this case, white could set up a ladder and reduce his losses as shown here, although black would get to play 5 and 7 and grab quite a few points of territory.

Figure 27. White 1 tries to make life for his group and also slide into what could become considerable black territory. How should black answer this?

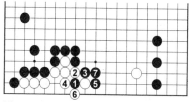

Figure 28. A forced sequence.

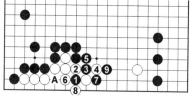

Figure 29. A dangerous variation.

Figure 28. Again, striking at the waist of the keima is the key. Moves 1 through 7 are forced, and black gets to close off the lower right.

Figure 29. White may atari at 4 to introduce some aji into the black position, but this could be dangerous if black chooses to answer 4 with **A**. In that case, white has to capture at 5, and black plays atari with 6 then grabs the three white stones to the left after white connects. White now has to take care of his group in an area where all the black stones are quite strong – not a good result at all.

Don't push through the keima.

This proverb advises against pushing through the knight's move at the wrong point (this is called a raw push). Be sure to consider both points in a keima's waist before cutting.

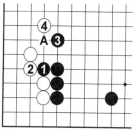

Figure 30. A raw push.

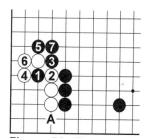

Figure 31. The correct way to cut.

Figure 30. This position arises from a joseki that white has not finished (by playing at **A**). Black 1 fails to take advantage of the defect in white's shape. The exchange of 3 and 4 gives white a good position.

Figure 31. (last page) This black 1 strikes at the waist of the keima correctly. White can't extend with 4 at 5, as black **A** would cause a large loss in the corner. (Black **A** is still a large end game move, though.)

Play the kosumi against the keima.

This often-quoted proverb describes the relationship between the keima and the kosumi, or diagonal move. A kosumi prevents your opponent from pressing at the same point and sets up a keima of its own to press down the opponent's stone.

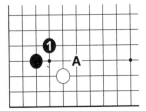

Figure 32. Play the kosumi against the knight's move.

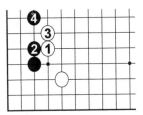

Figure 33. The pressing move is sente.

Figure 32. The kosumi of 1 is a standard answer to the knight's approach. Of course, we can't say that it takes more territory than a pincer since there are so many possibilities, but it is a very steady move that threatens to press at **A** next.

Figure 33. Often the kosumi is played simply to prevent the opponent from pressing with 1 and 3, which can be very strong if white has thickness to the right. Play these two sequences out on a board and you'll be amazed at the difference between them.

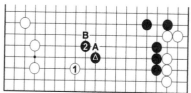

Figure 34. A great kosumi.

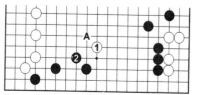

Figure 35. Defense and attack.

Figure 34. The kosumi from the marked stone on the fourth line can be very effective in strengthening the black moyo and reducing the white one (imagine a white play at 2, followed by black **A** then white **B** – white's territorial framework then rivals black's, and black's is open at the bottom on both sides).

Figure 35. This is the same idea in another position. White has played at 1 to reduce black's framework and black has answered accordingly. If white plays elsewhere, black **A** would be severe. Black's first priority here is to prevent white from pressing at 2.

Figure 36. Defending with black 1 is too greedy, as white immediately forces with 2 and closes with 4. Now it is white who has center influence. The diagonal move of the last figure was absolutely necessary.

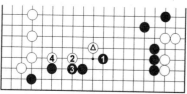

Figure 36. Punishing black's greed.

Answer the capping play with the keima.

The most common answer to the capping play is the keima, or knight's move. Of course there are other responses, such as stretching up to attach to the capping stone, attaching to the side of it, or playing somewhere else. (For an alternative to the capping play, see "Reduce a moyo gently with a shoulder hit or capping play".)

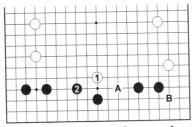

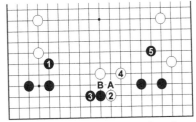

Figure 37. Answer the capping play with the keima.

Figure 38. You might also ignore the capping move.

Figure 37. Black answers the capping play of 1 by jumping to the side with the knight's move of 2 (note that he doesn't make the keima on the other side with **A** because the right corner can be invaded at **B**).

Figure 38. In this case, black can answer the capping play indirectly by jumping with 1. White will play 2 and 4 to settle himself, giving black a chance to take profit with 3. Notice that white has to have a favorable ladder for 2 and 4 to work, otherwise black will hane on top with **A** followed by white **B**, then black at 3.

The turning move is worth a lot.

Making a tight turn around an opponent's stone is worth quite a bit, especially if it reduces his moyo or enlarges your own. The turn is often so big that it is the only point on the board.

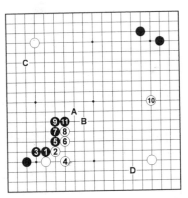

Figure 39. The turning move of 11 is bigger than it looks – in fact, it is the only move in this position, taken from an amateur game. Black displays his true strength with this move. Despite the proverb "Don't push along the fifth or sixth lines,

Figure 39. Turning with 11 is huge.

moves 1 through 9 give an even result – black's thickness is reduced by one white hoshi stone and white's wall is enhanced by the other.

Unfortunately, white lost his nerve and took the big point of 10 when he should have jumped ahead with **A**.

Black's turn at 11 is magnificent! It opens many possibilities: the jump to **B**, and the approach moves at **C** and **D** for example. These would all be more difficult if white played the keima at **A** instead of 10.

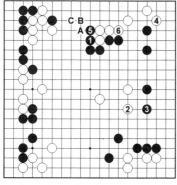

Figure 40. From a professional game.

Figure 40. Here's an example from a professional game in which, again, the turn of 1 is the only move to consider. White exchanges 2 for 3 to strengthen his two stones in the center, then takes the big move of 4.

(Notice that white leaves the upper-left side alone for now – his groups are strong enough to take care of themselves for the moment. If white plays 5 himself, black will tighten the noose with the sequence of **A**, **B**, and **C**.)

After black plays 5, white protects the upper side with 6 and black's turn of 5 has become very efficient.

Play hane at the head of two stones.
Play hane at the head of three stones.

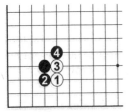

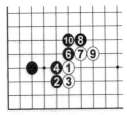

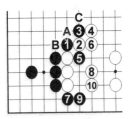

Figure 41. Black 4 strikes at the head of two stones.

Figure 42. Pressing the advantage.

Figure 43. Hane at the head of three stones.

Figure 41. There are a few people who approach the star point with the horrible move of 1. They aren't stupid (they play go, after all), so why do they do it? The move is easily refuted by this proverb– so maybe it's a psychological ploy. . . .

Black of course blocks with 2, and white's response at 3 is natural, but then black gets to play a hane at the head of the two stones, just as the proverb says. Already black has given his stones good shape, and white's stones will come under severe attack.

Figure 42. Moves 1 through 4 here are joseki, but white has played 5 elsewhere for some reason. This gives black the chance to play a hane at the head of two stones (where white should have played), then another hane at 8. By move 10, black has solid territory and some thickness. White has lost a lot here by breaking off the joseki.

Figure 43. Black 1 is a hane played at the head of three stones, as the second proverb directs. Through white 10, black has had it all his own way and not much of white's original territory remains. After this, black will play **A** to prevent white from doing so and making a double atari (where black would connect at **B** and white captures at **C**, making a valuable ponnuki).

Descend with the iron pillar.

The iron pillar is an extension to the third line from a stone on the fourth line (usually one of the side star points) and is a special-purpose move that prevents an enemy invader from making shape easily.

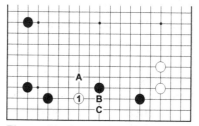

Figure 44. A popular invasion.

Figure 45. Black 1 is the iron pillar.

Figure 44. White 1 is a common way to invade this black framework, but it doesn't have much room to maneuver. White's primary concern will be to escape with good shape. Black's next move to attack the stones will be crucial to the development of the rest of his game.

Black has several options and must choose his attack carefully. One possibility is to play **A**, let white make a small life, and convert some of the black thickness into territory. White's responses include **B** and **C**.

Figure 45. Another possibility is this black move, called the iron pillar. It is very effective here, taking away white's chance to establish a base for his stone, and helping the black stone to the right. White will probably run toward the center to seek life, and black will be free to harass the escaping stones – moves 3, 5, and 7 are a profitable way to chase the invaders.

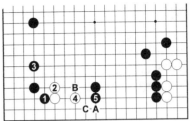

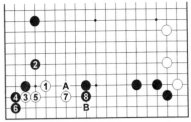

Figure 46. Example 2 of the iron pillar.

Figure 47. And a third example.

Figure 46. This position results from the sanrensei opening. White has finally invaded the huge black framework and black presses the attack with 1 and 3, a standard combination, then delivers the final punch with the iron pillar of 5, which prevents white's slide at **A**.

White could also play 4 high, at **B**, to which black would answer 5. In addition, black 5 could be at **C** in the basic diagram.

Figure 47. This position is based on the high Chinese opening, and white 1 to 7 are a standard pattern (white 7 could be played high at **A**). Black 8 prevents the slide at **B**.

Chapter 2
Good Shape and Bad

Don't make empty triangles.

Of all the bad shapes that may appear in a go game, the empty triangle is surely one of the worst. We single out the empty triangle because it is seen so often in amateur games and yet is so obviously inefficient. If you find yourself thinking of making one, read out the position more carefully – there's probably a better sequence.

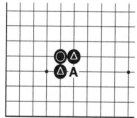

Figure 1. The basic empty triangle.

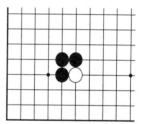

Figure 2. Not an empty triangle.

Figure 1. This shape is the basic empty triangle. It is the "circle" stone that makes the shape empty – its purpose in connecting the "triangle" stones is already being done by point **A** so playing it has been a waste of time.

Figure 2. Note that the black stones in this figure do not form an empty triangle. There's now a white stone at point **A** in the previous diagram, which makes black's shape good in this position (the stone that was unnecessary in Figure 1 now serves a purpose).

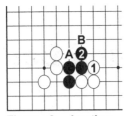

Figure 3. Another
empty triangle.

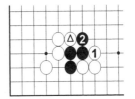

Figure 4. No empty
triangles here.

Figure 3. Because **A** is unoccupied, these black stones form an empty triangle. Black must jump out with **B** rather than plod step by step with moves like 2.

Figure 4. This black 2, as you may have guessed, does not produce an empty triangle because of the marked white stone – black's reply is absolutely necessary. There is clearly nothing wrong with this shape – neither black triangle is empty and all the stones are working with maximum efficiency.

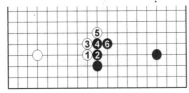

Figure 5. Pushing is good, but–

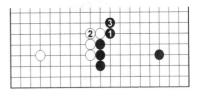

Figure 6. A much better idea.

Figure 5. Against the shoulder hit of 1, black pushes up with 2 and 4. All the moves are reasonable up to this point but, when white comes on top with 5, black gets scared and makes an empty triangle with 6. It's enough to make you cry.

Figure 6. Black has to play hane with 1 here (or cut off white's stone if he is confident of his fighting ability). Black should stretch to 3 in response to 2 – there is no reason to fear a cut. The superiority of this position over that in the last figure is obvious.

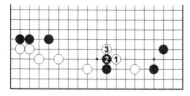

Figure 7 Another example.

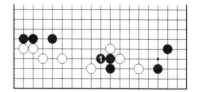

Figure 8. Don't do this!

Figure 7. In this figure, black has boldly invaded white's position and white has attacked with a knight's move then a hane (white can't ignore this affront, since another black move here will make the single white stone look like a deep invasion, that is, an overplay). How would you respond here?

Figure 8. By now, you surely have a feeling why you should avoid making empty triangles. White's blockade here is frightening. Can you find an alternative to avoid this?

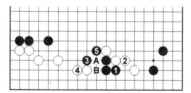

Figure 9. Do this instead!

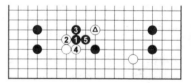

Figure 10. A common position in handicap go.

Figure 9. White is hoping that black will make an empty triangle, but black first dodges by turning at 1 then attaching with 3. Beginners may worry about white's wedging in at **A** and cutting off black 3, but this is easily refuted by black **B** then white 5 and black 4 (atari).

Continuing from the original sequence, white has to draw back with 4, which allows black to swell out at 5 and gain some sort of eye shape and an escape into the center.

Figure 10 (last page). White's cap with the marked stone is a grandiose strategy often seen in handicap go. Black should not be afraid to move out with 1. Unfortunately, black 1, 3, and 5 form an empty triangle. The rest of this section will examine, perhaps surprisingly, how black can move out into the center with good shape.

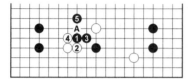

Figure 11. Bad for white.

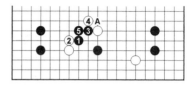

Figure 12. A standard sequence.

Figure 11. White has to be careful of the order of his moves. If he starts with 2 as above, black will pull back and connect with 3. Continuing with white 4 allows black to jump into the center with 5, which is much better than **A** (3 of Figure 10). Before looking at the next diagram, can you figure out what black should do if white pushes at 4 first?

Figure 12. Surprisingly, the empty triangle formed by moves 1, 3, and 5 is quite good here because of the potential cut left at **A**. This result is far better then that of Figure 10 because of the local distribution of white's stones – and an excellent example of why you should not follow proverbs blindly, an admonition that you should keep mind throughout the book.

Still, by now you understand why the empty triangle is such a bad shape and will avoid any moves that will lead you to making one. If you can force your opponent to make an empty triangle, you may find yourself playing a won game. On the other hand, don't get so caught up in the excitement that you end up having to make one yourself.

Don't make the soldier's helmet.

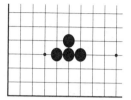

Figure 13. The soldier's helmet.

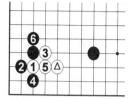

Figure 14. Afraid of ko.

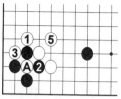

Figure 15. The correct joseki

Figure 13. This is the soldier's helmet, another classic bad shape. It looks like an empty triangle with a stone added in a not very useful place and, in fact, consists of two empty triangles.

Figure 14. Moves 1 through 4 are the beginning of the tsukefukure joseki, but the connection of white 5 is excruciatingly bad because it makes the soldier's helmet with the marked stone.

Figure 15. The only reason white could have had for connecting in the last diagram was the fear of a possible ko. White really has to atari with 1. After black takes with 2, white should atari again with 3. There is no reason for black to play this ko (and probably no way of winning it this early in the game), so he will connect, and white fixes up his shape with 5 to end the joseki.

Don't make dumpling shapes.

Clumps of stones with little eye-making ability are called "dumplings" in Japanese because of their compact shape (and perhaps because of the knot in your stomach when you encounter a bad one). These compact groups of stones can come under severe attack and are a burden to save. Their real disadvantage is that, for each stone in the clump, your opponent has played one that is either taking territory or radiating influence and you have nothing to show for it.

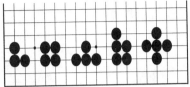

Figure 16. Five basic "dumpling" shapes.

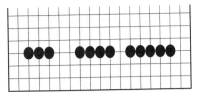

Figure 17. A more efficient distribution of stones.

Figure 16. These are the five basic dumpling shapes, which you should avoid making whenever possible. Two of them have names: the first from the left is known as an empty triangle; the third is the soldier's helmet.

Figure 17. Here, for comparison, are the stones rearranged in a straight line. Notice how much more territory each line can take than its clumsy counterpart and how much more influence each has. Also, the empty triangle has seven liberties to the straight three's eight; the four-stone groups have eight versus ten; and the five-stones groups, eight or nine versus twelve.

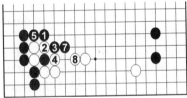

Figure 18. White makes a seven-stone dumpling.

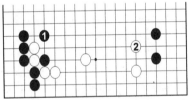

Figure 19. Avoid the clump and make a move with meaning!

Figure 18. Black 1 is a standard technique for building influence with sente. If white tries to protect his two stones with the sequence up to 8 (white 6 connects), he ends up with a clump of seven stones and has to take gote to protect them.

Figure 19. The two white stones aren't cutting stones or serving any good purpose, so white should instead play 2 here, a move that has real value. Black isn't going to take gote to take four or five points any time soon, and white has two peeps at these stones if he needs them later.

Exquisite moves can hide in bad shape.

Despite the warning against making any of the standard bad shapes, go positions can become very complex and sometimes you may have to play a vital point that happens to form a bad shape. Still, you should try to read out all other possibilities before making an empty triangle, a soldier's helmet, or a dumpling.

Ponnuki is worth thirty points.

The ponnuki shape is formed by capturing one enemy stone with four of your own and is said to be worth thirty points. The calculation is based on a ponnuki in the center of the board and is worth less the closer the shape is to the side. This is because part of its value is the result of the influence it radiates, which is of maximum benefit at the center of the board.

Nevertheless, you should not hesitate to make a ponnuki any time you have the chance. It is an excellent idea anywhere on the board.

The tortoise shell is worth sixty points.

Figure 20. The black stones, after capturing 1 and 5, form the shape called the tortoise shell, which is said to be worth sixty points. This may be an exaggeration, but modern professionals still put the value of this shape at almost fifty points so you should be happy to make one. (Black 8 is called the tail of the tortoise, by the way.)

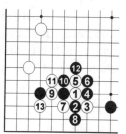

Figure 20. The tortoise shell shape.

Of course, black doesn't realize all these points as territory right away. The estimate is also based on the influence that the tortoise shell radiates and on the fact that the black stones are now alive and very strong.

Play at the center of three stones.

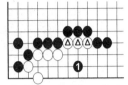

Figure 21. The vital point.

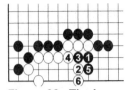

Figure 22. The hane doesn't work well.

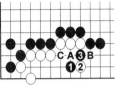

Figure 23. White is in a tough spot.

Figure 21. Black 1 strikes at the center of the three marked stones. Because the stones have only three liberties, black 1 is the vital point.

Figure 22. This black 1 is clearly inferior to the move in the previous figure. In other circumstances, it might be the vital point, but not here. White is happy, safe, and snug.

Figure 23. Black 1 and 3 utilize white's shortage of liberties perfectly. An atari at **A** is impossible, and an atari at **B** forces black to capture the three stones at **C** in a snap-back.

Figure 24. White 2 and 4 are correct and give the white group life. (Black can play 3 at 4, but white will answer at **A**; black 5 at **B** captures one stone but white lives with a play between 3 and 5 in the figure.) Black 5 captures three stones and is also sente against the remainder of the white group.

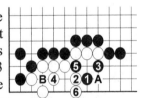

Figure 24. White 2 is the correct answer.

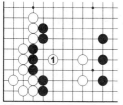
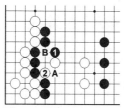
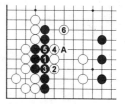

Figure 25. Another example.

Figure 26. Black takes a loss.

Figure 27. This is even worse.

Figure 25. Black has not paid attention to the shape of his stones and white 1 strikes at the key point.

Figure 26. If black tries the loose connection of 1, the weakness of the three stones becomes apparent (black 1 at **A** instead is of course answered by **B)**. Black has been caught in a classic shortage of liberties and has no good answer.

Figure 27. Black may try to kill two birds with one stone by connecting with 1 here, but this is much worse. White simply peeps at 2 and 4, then jumps at 6, and now it is black's stones that come under a severe attack. On the other hand, black may answer with a solid connection at 3, but white will play **A**, followed by black 5 at 4. This doesn't seem any good either.

Figure 28. If white fails to take advantage of black's bad shape and instead jumps to 1, black must take the vital point himself with 2 to defend his group. White has missed a golden opportunity – just compare this figure to the last to see the difference.

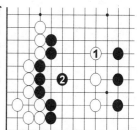

Figure 28. Missing an opportunity.

Don't let your stones be cut completely.

Allowing your stones to be cut through completely can lose you more than you might think. Normally this arises when you ignore a peep at your one-point jump, but it can occur elsewhere as well.

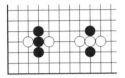

Figure 29. Compare the two positions.

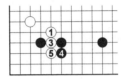

Figure 30. Black is completely cut.

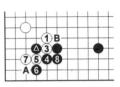

Figure 31. Resist being cut through.

Figure 29. These two positions show how much weaker stones are when they are separated. The three connected stones in each case have no worries at all, while the separated stones have no hope.

Figure 30. White has played 1 as a ko threat, which was ignored, then continued with 3. Black, thoroughly cowed, makes the heavy move at 4 so white is quite happy to take a large corner. Black simply can't play this way!

Figure 31. Black must block the push with 4 here. White will probably cut with 5 here and the moves to 8 follow. Black can still get some use out of the marked stone as both **A** and **B** are sente.

Figure 32. White should have jumped to 1 himself in this position but he didn't, so black got the chance to cap the white stone. Coming out with 2 is the only move, then black continued by forcing white out into the center.

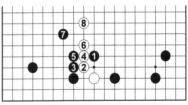

Figure 32. A common position, but the wrong answer.

Black 3 through 7 are a bad choice of moves – white is out of danger, and the black stones on the left are badly overconcentrated. The fact that black 1 and 5 have been cut through should have warned black that this sequence was unfavorable.

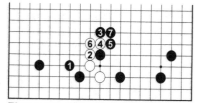

Figure 33. This is better, but. . . .

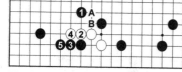

Figure 34. The correct answer.

Figure 33. Since black 3 in the previous figure was at fault, black may try a diagonal move instead. Jumping out with 3 is good, and the remaining moves are all standard. But black can do even better.

Figure 34. Following the proverb "Attack with the keima," black should play 1. This makes white force black to take solid territory with 3 and 5. Black could also have played **A** with 1; both moves build nice central influence. Notice that pushing white along with black **B** and so on would be the same as Figure 32, except that it would be the 8–3 stone that suffers.

Don't peep at a bamboo joint.
A bamboo joint can't be cut.

Figure 35 shows the standard bamboo joint, formed by the original white stone and white 1, 3, and 5. This formation provides a very strong connection – white would have to ignore a move for black to cut through. But, for some reason, many people play moves that end up peeping at a bamboo joint. This can be a sign that their groups have bad shape.

Figure 35. In this figure, black has peeped twice at a bamboo joint with 4 and 6. Although black 4 has some use in preventing a cut to the left of 2, 6 is clearly bad shape and should have been a kosumi at **A**.

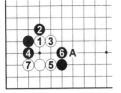

Figure 35. The bamboo joint, a common shape.

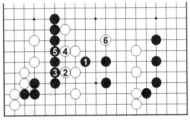

Figure 36. Don't peep at a bamboo joint!

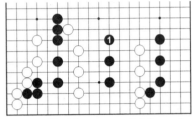

Figure 37. The one-point jump is correct.

Figure 36. Black has carelessly peeped at 1, forcing white to make a bamboo joint in sente. This gives white the chance to start a severe attack with 6.

Figure 37. Black's only good move in this position is the one-point jump at 1. This gets his stones out into the center where they can survive.

Don't make the bottle shape.

Figure 38. Black, fearing complications, jumps out with the knight's move of 1 – the three stones form what is known as the bottle shape (or the dog's face). The bottle shape should be avoided because of the inefficient use of the stones, even though it seems to be popular. Black then continues with 3 to keep from being closed in.

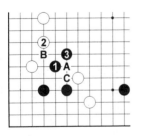

Figure 38. Avoid this.

Instead of 1, black must move out quickly with **A**. White should answer with **B**, to which black will respond by connecting at **C**. It is bad for white to try to cut off **A** right away, since black can counter by attaching to the weak white stone at the left, just below **B**.

Attach at the 3–3 point to make shape.

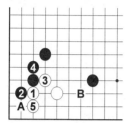

Figure 39. Attach to make shape.

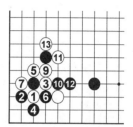

Figure 40. Here's a variation.

Figure 39. White has allowed black to play three stones to his one in this area, and he wants to settle himself here as quickly as possible. The last thing he wants is to start a fight in which black's superior forces have the advantage.

The answer is to attach at the 3–3 point with 1. The sequence to 5 settles white's group for the moment, though it is important to remember that **A** and **B** are miai. If black takes one, white must take the other to keep his group from becoming a target.

Figure 40. Instead of going for territory along the left side, black may opt for the corner as shown here. After white plays atari at 7, black connects at 8 since, as the saying goes, there is no ko in the opening. This variation is fair to both sides, considering that black had two extra stones in the area to start with.

Attach to make shape.

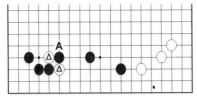

Figure 41. White to play.

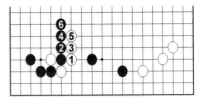

Figure 42. Brute force fails.

Figure 41. This sort of position, in which you have to reduce an area where the opponent is fairly strong, is common in actual play. If black gets the chance to play **A**, the situation will become quite difficult for white. Using the aji of the two marked stones as efficiently as possible, how should white deal with the black framework?

Figure 42. The atari of 1 and continuing to push toward the center is probably the first idea that occurs to most people, but black is one step ahead in the moves toward the center. This is bad enough, but he is also gaining an increasing hold on a nice piece of territory on the left. The threat to the two black stones by the new white wall isn't nearly enough to compensate for this.

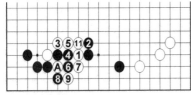

Figure 43. Attach!

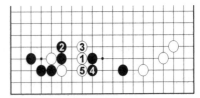

Figure 44. Black counters, but –

Figure 43. The attachment of 1 is the vital point for making shape here. If black stands with 2 to strengthen his position on the right, white has a beautiful forcing sequence with 3 through 9 (black connects with 10), and after the connection of 11 white has no worries at all.

Figure 44. Black may extend to 2 here, but then white can simply extend as well and, if black descends at 4 to protect his two stones, white plays 5 to deprive black of an easy connection and to set up a tentative base for his stones. Both are settled for the moment, but the future for both groups lies in the center of the board.

Attach and crosscut to make shape.

Figure 45. Here, white has just invaded, threatening to undercut the stone to the right, and black responded by capping the invader. The attachment and crosscut are perfect in this situation. If white instead tries to escape with **A**, black will begin a leaning attack at **B** which will be hard on white.

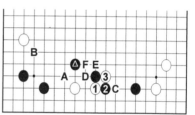

Figure 45. A magnificent combination for making shape.

If black simply pulls back with **C**, after the crosscut, white will be happy to initiate the sequence **D**, **E**, and **F** and escape into the center.

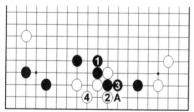

Figure 46. The continuation.

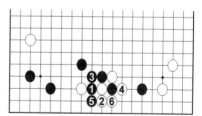

Figure 47. Another variation.

Figure 46. Extending with black 1 is a solid way to play and quite common. Black expects white to settle himself with 2 through 4, although 4 may be played at **A**.

Figure 47 (last page). An atari with 1 is another way to play and this figure shows a reasonable exchange: black gets the left and white, the right. White 4 might also be played at 5, but the sequence shown is acceptable to both sides.

Chapter 3
Playing Ko

If you're afraid of ko, don't play go.

To the average amateur, fighting an important ko can be a terrifying experience. You will often see weaker players who, backing off from starting a ko, take a loss in territory or give up a promising fight, and this is contrary to the spirit of the game.

To become a dan player, you must embrace the concept of ko and make it an active part of your repertoire. Many of the positions that come up in a game are alive or dead by ko. Instead of trying to avoid a ko, try to see how you can start one to your opponent's disadvantage.

There is no ko at the beginning of the game.

This proverb says that, at the very beginning of a game, there are no ko threats large enough to justify starting a ko fight. If your opponent does start one, just ignore the threat and take the ko.

Figure 1. Wanting to start hand-to-hand combat quickly in this nine-stone game, white sets up a ko in the lower right corner.

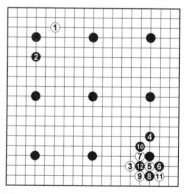

Figure 1. Starting a ko in a nine-stone game.

Figure 2. The best ko threat white can come up with is 1, and it's not nearly enough (besides which, black has no ko threat for his next move). Black of course takes the ko with 2.

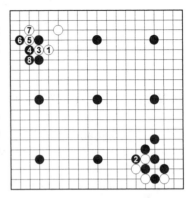

After the sequence shown, white has perhaps twelve or thirteen points while black has taken a solid twenty-five or thirty.

Figure 2. Ignore the ko threat.

Start with the smallest ko threat that works.

This is just common sense, but you see time and time again players beginning a ko fight by using the biggest threat they can find, then making progressively smaller ones as the fight goes on. This is such a waste.

Always start with the smallest ko threat that is larger than the value of the ko, then work up in value as necessary. Save your biggest ko threats for the most important ko fights later on. Of course, the size of a ko threat isn't always easy to count – your opponent may threaten to set up another ko somewhere else, or he may threaten to cut off a group that isn't clearly alive on its own – but you'll find that such calculations become easier with practice.

Use your dead groups for ko threats.

If you find that you are one move behind in a race to capture, it's important to stop playing in that area and conserve your resources. Resist the desire to play a move on the outside just to gain a point of territory. A group that your opponent has killed but not yet taken off the board can be a great source of ko threats, and the earlier that you stop playing there the more ko threats you will have.

Adjacent ko threats can win the fight.

Ko threats are said to be adjacent to a ko fight if they directly affect the stones under attack. Such ko threats include the possibility of capturing some of the surrounding stones, connecting to the outside, and making eyes.

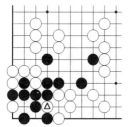

Figure 3. Look for adjacent ko threats.

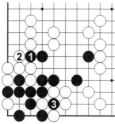

Figure 4. The first of many ko threats.

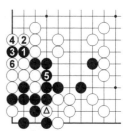

Figure 5. A few more ko threats.

Figure 3. Here's a position in which white has just taken a ko with the marked stone. Black needs to win the ko, kill something, make another eye, or escape to the center.

Figure 4. Black 1 is an adjacent ko threat because it threatens to capture five of the stones surrounding the black group and make a big eye. White of course answers with 2 and black takes the ko with 3.

Figure 5. Figures 5 and 6 use a graphical shorthand here so that the whole ko fight will fit into a reasonable amount of space: each black-white exchange represents black's ko threat, white's answer, black taking the ko, white making a ko threat somewhere else on the board, black answering it, and white retaking the ko.

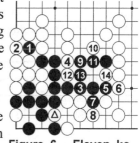

Figure 6. This figure shows seven more adjacent ko threats for black, a total of eleven (there is even another to the right of 8).

Figure 6. Eleven ko threats altogether!

Be careful using adjacent ko threats.

This proverb is another reminder that you must not follow the advice given in this book blindly.

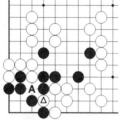

Figure 7. Black to play.

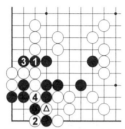

Figure 8. Too much of a hurry.

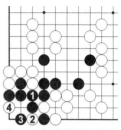

Figure 9. Still dead.

Figure 7.   This position is the same as the one given for the last proverb except that the stone at **A** has not been played and the corner is missing one black stone and one white one. Where should black play?

Figure 8. If black thinks to play the ko using 1 as a ko threat, as he did in the previous example, his group will die very quickly.

Figure 9. Should black try to fix his defect directly, his group dies in an equally embarrassing debacle.

Figure 10. Since this **A** doesn't work yet, the only way to live is by ko, starting with 1. White connects at 2, so black plays at the vital 1–2 point then white retakes the ko with 4 (**B**).

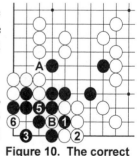

Black plays 5, hoping to make two eyes at 6, but white plays there next and the ko becomes a fight for life. The adjacent ko threats starting with **A** now come in very handy.

Figure 10. The correct play.

Don't play ko threats that hurt you.

There is a tendency among amateurs to make ko threats that cost them points, and this must be avoided whenever possible.

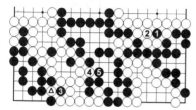

Figure 11. Starting a ko fight.

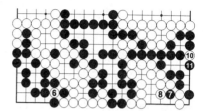

Figure 12. The continuation.
9 @ A

Figures 11 and 12. White has just taken the ko at the bottom with the marked stone and the fight continues through white 12, which retakes the ko. So far, all the moves are reasonable.

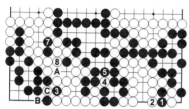

Figure 13. A few more moves.
6 @ C

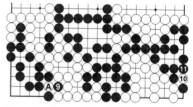

Figure 14. The conclusion.
12 @ A

Figures 13 and 14. The first harmful ko threat is black 1. White has to take the other black stone here anyway, so this just gives away a free point. Consider that white would have had seven points in this area without black 1; including the capture of black 1, white now has eight points.

The next bad ko threat was black 7. After the ko fight, white would have had to play **A** or 8, but black 7 forces 8 and gives white another free point.

The fact is that, even if black wins the ko, he gains only two points (the captured stone plus **B**) so the best he can hope for is to break even.

Count your threats before starting a ko.

This is another common-sense precaution that many players fail to take. Before starting a fight that you can see will center on a ko, estimate the size of the ko and count the number of threats that each of you has that apply to the situation. If you have fewer than your opponent, look for some way to avoid the ko without giving away too much in the fight.

PART II

THE EARLY GAME

Chapter 4
The Opening

Play the first move in your upper right corner.

In even games, black traditionally plays the first move in his upper right corner as a sign of respect for his opponent. This courtesy allows white to either play near the black stone or in an adjacent corner without the trouble of reaching across the board.

The traditional order of play in the opening: (1) first a move in an empty corner; (2) a shimari or approach move; (3) an extension along the side; then (4) a jump into the center last.

This proverb states the traditional order of play in the opening. If there is an empty corner, play there first, where it is easiest to make territory. If there are no empty corners, play a second move in a corner – a shimari if you back up one of your own stones to make an enclosure, or a kakari if you approach one of your opponent's stones.

When all the corners have been settled, making an extension along one of the sides will be the biggest move on the board. Jumping into the center should be among the last big moves played in the opening.

You can't really go wrong following traditional wisdom, but it is hardly absolute – for example, there is the success of the Chinese and sanrensei openings, in which black plays his third move on the side between his first two stones rather than approaching an opponent's stone. As with most proverbs, this saying should not be followed blindly – rather, use it as a guide to help find the best move on the board.

Be first to play in front of a shimari.

After all the corners have been occupied, the biggest move on the board is a play in front of a shimari, or enclosure (either your own or the opponent's). The largest of these is a move that establishes or interferes with a double-wing structure (see "The stork's wing formation"). Of lesser value, but still big, are extensions made to the side of a shimari, but these are clearly secondary to an extension in front of one.

Respond with the three-space extension.

Extending three spaces from a stone with an extra-large knight's move, as shown below, is a light way to play that stresses quick development. It forms a flexible group that is stronger than it looks.

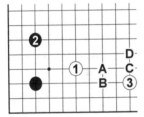

Figure 1. The extra-large knight's move.

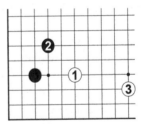

Figure 2. Another popular joseki.

Figures 1 and 2. Here are two josekis that make use of the extra-large knight's move, also called the ōgeima. White 3 is played when it is also a good extension from a white position in the lower right.

Of course black can invade these positions, but all continuations are easy for white. If black plays **A**, white plays **B** and vice-versa. Normally, though, you can expect black to apply pressure from above with **D**, to which white can answer with any of **A** through **C** or a move on the right, depending on the circumstances.

Note that playing white 3 on the fourth line makes it too easy for the opponent to break the light connection between the two white stones.

If high on one side, play low on the other.
If low on one side, play high on the other.

This proverb describes the important balance between the third and fourth lines, especially when making an extension along the side. When extending from a fourth-line stone or group, play on the third line and vice-versa.

By the way, there is rarely anything wrong with extending two spaces on the third line to make a base for a single stone. But you often see two-space extensions one after the other, all on the third line – this "lantern procession" is very bad. While a player is taking such a low position, their opponent has most likely built up overwhelming influence or taken profit somewhere else.

Also dangerous is the delusion that the loose string cannot be cut (it can, just attach at the side of one of the center stones and cross-cut).

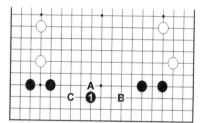

Figure 3. A balanced position.

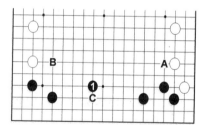

Figure 4. Nice sense of balance.

Figure 3. Because black has high positions in both of the bottom corners, playing 1 on the third line gives a beautiful, balanced position. Playing high at **A**, though, would invite an immediate invasion at **B** or **C** to take advantage of the weakness of the high position.

Figure 4 (last page). This time black is low on both sides, so a play on the fourth line is called for to establish a balanced position. Black can then continue swelling up this moyo by playing **A** or **B**, which would be considerably less profitable if 1 had been played low at **C** instead.

Try to make the stork's wing formation.

The stork's wing formation is so named because, if a shimari is considered the body of a stork, the wide extensions to either side resemble its wings. This is possibly the most desirable arrangement of four stones you can have in the opening.

Figure 5. The stork's wing formation is based on the ikken, or one-space, shimari in the upper right corner and maps out potential territory along the right and upper sides. This shimari (like a stone on the star point) allows a full extension down the side. Wide extensions from both sides of other corner positions are called double-wing formations.

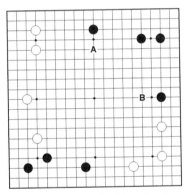

Figure 5. The stork's wing formation is ideal.

If black can add a stone at **A** or **B**, the structure becomes truly imposing and white will have a hard time reducing it enough to have any chance of winning.

The butterfly formation is bad.

Figure 6. When there is already a large knight's move from the star point, an extension to the marked black stone (making the butterfly, or Kwannon, formation) is considered very bad because it is open to an invasion at the 3–3 point.

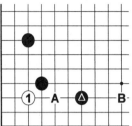

Figure 6. The Kwannon formation is very bad!

The purpose of making the first large knight's move from the star point is to take the corner with **A** if the opponent doesn't get the chance to invade first. Equally important, if he does invade, you get powerful outside influence when you seal him in. So it follows that you want to extend as far as **B** if you can.

Welcome the invasion at the 3–3 point.

This proverb restates the desirability of making wide extensions from stones on the star point, mentioned in the last proverb. Many players worry about the 3–3 invasion when they should welcome it. Invading at the 3–3 point gives the other side considerable thickness, so you should play outside first to nullify this potential.

The truth is that a stone on the star point is ideally situated to build thickness in the center but it is weak at surrounding territory directly. Indeed, you want to emphasize the star point's superiority in influence to gain an even bigger advantage – trying instead to force your stone to do something that it doesn't do very well misses a valuable opportunity.

People who insist on adding stones near a star point to take immediate territory are really working to defeat themselves and probably should not be playing on the star point until they understand it better. (Taking a handicap is great incentive to learning to use thickness properly.)

In addition, the star point also has the advantage of handling the corner with one move, which is very important early in the opening, so wide extensions are best for fast development.

Since the 3–3 invasion invariably forces the star point to make powerful outside thickness, you should welcome the invasion and plan your whole-board strategy to make the most of one.

Here are some examples. (Note that invasions are usually preceded by an approach move, otherwise the outside thickness that black builds will be so overwhelming that white will have trouble finding any chance to win.)

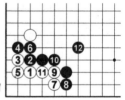

Figure 7. Invading the hoshi-keima enclosure.

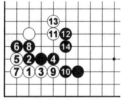

Figure 8. Invading the hoshi - ogeima enclosure.

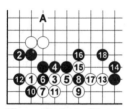

Figure 9. Invading a larger enclosure.

Figure 7. Even with the tight keima to back it up, the star point can be invaded. White's life in the corner is worth so much less than black's solid walls that he should be wary of this exchange under almost any circumstances.

Figure 8. Invading the enclosure made with the ogeima, or large-knight move, is more interesting for white. The rhythm of the stones allows him to continue on the outside with 11 and 13 to reduce black's influence somewhat.

Figure 9. Black is threatening to solidify a rather large area on the side here, so white invades at the 3–3 point. Black gets little territory in the corner, but a black stone somewhere in the direction of **A** would work exceedingly well with his thickness.

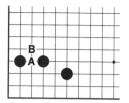

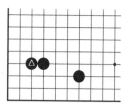

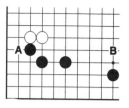

Figure 10. Protecting the keima.

Figure 11. Protecting the ogeima.

Figure 12. Only partial protection.

Figure 10. If black has the chance to add another stone to the hoshi-keima enclosure, he should jump down to close his corner (or play **A** or **B**, which are equally effective).

Figure 11. The hoshi-ogeima enclosure needs the move shown by the marked stone to be secure. Black has taken nearly twenty points of territory, but it has taken three stones to do it. Bear this in mind when weighing alternatives elsewhere on the board.

Figure 12. To claim the corner territory in this position, you should play at **A**. Because the extension on the right is so wide, there is room for white to invade, attach, or reduce. If the right side is more important, you might consider playing at **B** instead and allow the 3–3 invasion, letting white connect to the two stones on the left.

Next is a position in which black has no choice but to defend his corner or die. Needless to say, black should never have let white play so many moves in this area without responding.

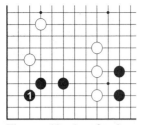

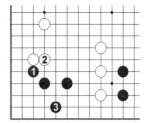

Figure 13. A safe de-
fense.

Figure 14. Another
way.

Figure 13. Black 1 prevents the 3–3 invasion directly. This is a very safe defense, but it allows white to slide in from either side.

Figure 14. If black dislikes being open at both sides, he can choose this alternative.

Play vital points before big points.

Vital points are moves that must be made to cover a weakness in your position. For example, taking a vital point may give your group good shape or life, prevent a forced entry into your moyo, or finish off a joseki.

There is a tendency among weaker players (and a few pathologically strong ones) to leave a vital point unplayed in order to rush off to take a big point or attack something. This may gain a temporary advantage but will usually come back to haunt the offender later on. Such impatience can only hurt one's game in the long run.

A good part of most dan-level openings involves competing for the strategically big points on the board. In general, there is nothing wrong with this approach, but it is more important to take the vital points as they appear in your game.

Don't play near thickness.

This proverb says that you must not play near strong stones, either your opponent's or your own. There is little to gain from doing so and you can easily take on more than you can handle – playing too near an opponent's strong group invites a severe, and unnecessary, attack that may cost you the game. On the other hand, playing too near to your own group wastes its potential by overconcentrating your stones and lowering their efficiency.

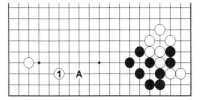

Figure 15. An honest extension.

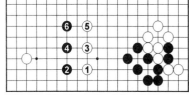

Figure 16. Very bad for white.

Figure 15. When faced with as much thickness as black has on the lower right, white can't really extend any further than 1 – it just leaves a hole in his position and gives up a profitable shimari. Next, black will probably play something like **A** to gain compensation for the territory that white took on the right side while black built his wall.

The black group looms over the lower side like a mountain and, as in real life, you can be hurt by falling stones if you approach too closely.

Figure 16. If white extends too far, black immediately counterattacks with 2, 4, and 6. Black has built new thickness in sente that threatens the single white stone at the left. Compare this result with black's playing at **A** in the last figure.

Figure 17. Even if white restrains himself with 1, a follow up at or near 3 is necessary to redeem the move, but this has no effect on the black group and is minimally profitable.

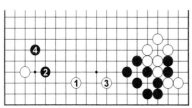

Figure 17. Still bad for white.

Meanwhile, black gets to play a second move against the corner at 4. Compared to the position in Figure 15, the loss white suffers is huge.

Figure 18. If it is black's turn, he wants to extend as far from his wall as possible, and the approach at 1 is ideal. Next white should play 2, which black will answer with 3.

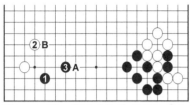

Figure 18. The ideal move for black.

White can't really pincer around **A** because after black plays **B**, both of white's stones are looking quite lonely and they will have a tough fight ahead of them.

Don't crawl any more than you have to.

Crawling on the second or third line in the opening is submissive and unprofitable. Each move on the second line gains you one point, while crawling on the third line only gains you two – hardly enough to compensate you for the wall that your opponent is building in the center. This is something you do only when you have to stabilize your group.

Figure 19. Moves 1 through 12 are a common joseki, which is perhaps acceptable in this position, but continuing with white **A**, black **B**, then **C** and **D** is very bad for white. Black just gets stronger and stronger on the outside, while white gains only one point for each time he crawls – these are small moves even in the end game. White is alive in the corner anyway so continuing this way is cutting one's own throat.

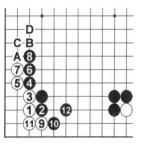

Figure 19. A common joseki.

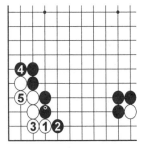

Figure 20. White 1 is a big mistake.

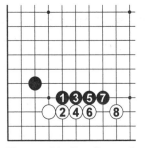

Figure 21. Don't crawl more than you have to.

Figure 20. A limited amount of crawling is needed to settle the white stones in sente, though. If white, trying too hard to avoid creeping along the third line, plays 1 instead of 4 in this figure, he is at a distinct disadvantage – black will play 2 and 4 in sente then play a big point somewhere else.

Figure 21. White doesn't know where this joseki ends – he seems happy to continue crawling along the third line, letting black build up additional thickness that is easily worth twice the few extra points white gains.

Figure 22. This is the correct way to play – white should crawl once at the marked stone then jump ahead. Even though black can push through at **A** and cut, white can settle his stones and is one step ahead in the chase along the side, so this is considered an even result. (It is more common for black to continue pushing white along the third line a little longer to build a little more thickness in the center.)

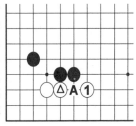

Figure 22. Crawl once, then jump ahead.

The second line is the line of defeat.
The third line is the line of territory.
The fourth line is the line of victory.

These proverbs refer to the efficiency of extending to the next intersection from an established group in the opening, usually when the enemy is pressing down from the line above.

Don't crawl along the second line unless you absolutely have to – you will hear this often throughout your go career. While there are times when it is necessary to do so, these are limited to cases where your stones are struggling for life or where your opponent can close off the side with a simultaneous threat to kill. If this is not true, don't crawl any further.

To stabilize a group on the third line, either extending or crawling will do the job. You'll be taking two points of territory with each crawl, and this is not terribly inferior to the thickness your opponent is building, but bear in mind the last proverb we covered, "Don't crawl any farther than you have to." It is important to consider the balance of territory and influence over the whole board before creeping along on the third line.

On the other hand, moving along the fourth line is an efficient way to take territory and you should not hesitate to do so. An exception would be when your opponent has built overwhelming thickness in the center of the board and you don't want to make it even harder to invade. Even then it may be a possible way to play.

Of course, the other player is unlikely to hand you fourth-line territory because of the proverb "Never push on the fifth or sixth line" but, if there are weaknesses in his position that will allow you to make a successful invasion, take the gift and smile gratefully.

Don't allow two pressing moves on the same side.

Figure 23. This figure shows why you must never let your opponent play two pressing moves on the same side – just compare white's two tiny positions on the side with black's powerful central influence. Moreover, black can continue to press at A and B.

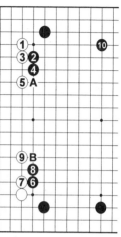

Figure 23. Never allow two pressing moves on one side.

White's mistake was in playing 1, which should have been at 6 to prevent a pressing move at the same point (and to threaten an invasion between the two black stones at the bottom).

If white feels a need to play against the upper left corner, the approach move at 2 is far better than 1.

Approach from the wider side.
Block on the wider side.

When playing against the 3–3 point or a star point with outposts on both sides, approach it from the widest, most open side. This gives your approach move more room to maneuver and also breaks up more of your opponent's framework. If, as is often the case, he responds with a play on the other side of the 3–3 or star point, he is surrounding the smaller of the two sides.

The second proverb explains how to block the 3–3 invasion under the star point. Blocking on the side that gives you the most potential territory is just common sense.

There are exceptions, of course. For example, it is usually not a good idea to block on a side with an open skirt regardless of the width of the position. Each situation is slightly different, and the best way to learn the exceptions to any proverb is to study games by professional go players.

Study the Shusaku opening.

Figure 24. The location and orientation of black 1, 3, and 5 are the hallmark of the Shusaku opening.

This opening has been analyzed extensively and should be included in every go player's study of opening theory.

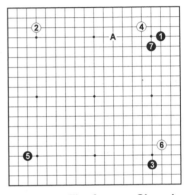

Honinbo Shusaku (1829–1862) was the first to systematically explore all of white's counters in a given opening position and thus laid the foundations of modern opening

Figure 24. The famous Shusaku opening.

theory. Shusaku built up an incredible series of wins using this technique over the years and so it has become known as the Shusaku opening.

Black ignored white 4 to play in the empty corner, then white naturally approached with 6. The big surprise came with the diagonal move of 7, which came to be called the Shusaku kosumi. Shusaku was so proud of this move that he often boasted that, as long as the game continued to be played on a 19-line board, his kosumi would never be a bad move.

Before the introduction of komi, that would probably have been true, but now that black has to win on the board by half a dozen points or so, Shusaku's kosumi is just too slow. Instead, the more positive pincer at A has become the usual reply to white 6. Although his kosumi is rarely played, Shusaku's opening is alive and doing well.

Chapter 5
Joseki

Memorize joseki to become weaker.
Study joseki to become stronger.

The first proverb warns against simple memorization of corner openings – without an understanding of why each move is played, this will do you more harm than good.

On the other hand, learning the reason behind each move and how the joseki works with the rest of the board can only make you stronger. By understanding the details, you are better able to refute unreasonable departures from the sequences you have learned.

Also, there are many ideas that you can't get from books. For example, the many undocumented "quasi-joseki" have to be learned through experience and studying the games of strong players. And sometimes a non-standard move leaves aji that is only slightly bad and can't be punished immediately without hurting your current position (these you leave alone for the moment and aim at in future fighting).

Studying joseki will teach you much more than just patterns you can follow. Its rewards include a better understanding of shape, tesuji, relative strengths of stones, and even end-game play.

The taisha joseki has a hundred variations.

The taisha is said to be the most complex joseki of all, with more than a hundred variations (although a thousand may be closer to the truth). A variety of complicated variations seem to spring from every move, and perhaps it takes the strength of professional shodan to say that one has mastered the taisha.

Figure 1. The taisha joseki arises from pressing with the large knight's move from the 3–5 point against a stone at 3–4. This figure shows perhaps the simplest, most often played variation. You would be well-advised to study a book devoted to the taisha (even in Japanese, Chinese, or Korean), before using the taisha in important games.

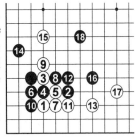

Figure 1. The taisha joseki.

Threaten a double atari.

When given the chance to atari, it is often better to set up a double atari instead and see how your opponent will respond.

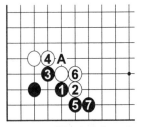

Figure 2. Black 5 threatens a double atari.

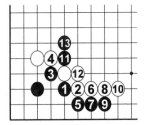

Figure 3. Punishing white for extending.

Figure 2. This joseki results from the knight's pressing move against the 3–3 invasion and nicely implements white's plan to build outside thickness (which is one of the aims of playing on the 3–5 point). After white blocks at 4, black has no time to atari at **A** with 5, so he sets up the double atari instead. If white defends with 6, black can stick out his head with 7. (Playing black 5 at 6 then making an atari on 2 next leaves bad aji for black and is not recommended.)

Figure 3. Connecting at 6 in the last diagram was the correct move. If white is greedy and continues with 6 through 10, black will settle his group than jump on the chance to atari with 11 and extend at 13 to start a promising fight.

Extend after the crosscut.

Figure 4. White attaches at 1 to the star-point enclosure when he doesn't want to invade at the 3–3 point and give black a lot of outside influence. The combination of white 1 and 3 is known as a crosscut, which can give rise to quite a few variations – on the next move, black can atari four ways or extend in four directions.

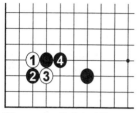

Figure 4. Extend from the crosscut!

This proverb cuts in half the number of variations that you have to read out: just consider the extensions and you won't get into too much trouble. Of course, there are situations where you should atari instead but, if you are rushed, this is a good rule of thumb.

Capture the cutting stone.

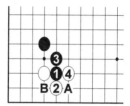

Figure 5. A cutting joseki.

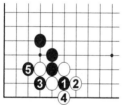

Figure 6. Variation 1: Taking the corner.

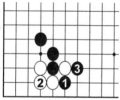

Figure 7. White 2 is bad.

Figure 5. This joseki leaves two cutting points, **A** and **B**, between which black must choose to finish the sequence. Black cuts at **A** if he wants the corner or at **B** if he wants outside influence.

Figure 6. In the normal continuation white captures with 2 (which is what this proverb is all about). Black gets the corner but white has sente and the option to build up thickness.

Figure 7 (last page). Connecting at 2 is bad because white gets a clump of stones with far less eye-making ability than if he had captured as in Figure 6.

Figure 8. Black cuts on the inside if he wants outside influence (be sure to check that the ladder is favorable before you play this joseki).

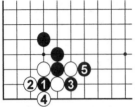

Figure 8. Variation 2: Choosing influence.

Crosscut, atari, then extend.

Figure 9. This proverb serves to remind you how to play the 4–5 joseki shown to the right. After the crosscut of white 4, black plays atari then extends. Usually white plays 8 then black captures white 4 in a ladder to build outside influence.

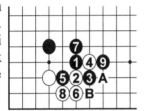

Figure 9. A 4–5 joseki.

Note that playing black 5 at 7 is bad. White will play **A**, black at 5, and white gets a ponnuki by capturing at **B**. (Ponnuki is the shape formed by capturing one stone as efficiently as possible [that is, with white 2, 4, **A**, and **B**]; ponnuki is so good that it is said to be worth thirty points!)

The plum-bowl shape is strong.

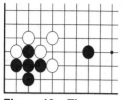

Figure 10. The corner black stones are the "plum bowl."

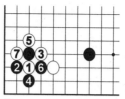

Figure 11. The tsuke-fukure joseki.

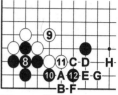

Figure 12. The continuation.

Figure 10. This is the "plum-bowl" shape, a name coined by the master of tsume-go, Maeda Nobuaki (1907 – 1975). It may look a little heavy, but it is quite strong.

Figures 11 and 12. Here is the tsukefukure joseki, which gives rise to the plum bowl shape. White plays 1 to settle his stones quickly by sacrificing the corner stone to get good shape. Black can't play ko here, and so fills at 8. White 9 makes excellent shape, and black usually continues by loosely connecting with 12 (note that white can cut with the sequence **A** through **G**, but then black just plays at **H** – still, this aji has to be kept in mind when playing in the lower right).

Make shape with the one-space diagonal jump.

Figure 13. The one-space diagonal jump of 1 is not an obvious response to the two-space high pincer, but it can be very useful and may help you surprise your opponents.

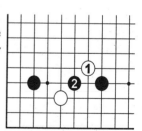

Figure 13. The one-space diagonal jump.

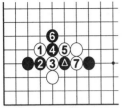

Figure 14. Making good shape.

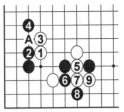

Figure 15. Another idea.

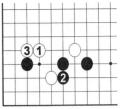

Figure 16. And yet another.

Figure 14. White plays 1 with the idea of sacrificing it in order to give the rest of his stones good shape. The exchange here has each player capturing an enemy stone and the situation is considered settled for now.

Figure 15. Black may consider answering the knight's press by crawling with 2 then jumping out with 4, but then white has the forcing moves of 5 through 9 and black's position on the right is in tatters. Black also has to watch out for white's push through at **A** then cut, so this sequence isn't really playable for black.

Figure 16. The solid drop of black 2 is quite strong and a good way to play. White is not dissatisfied either, so this is a fair exchange.

PART III

THE STONES GO WALKING

Chapter 6
Territorial Frameworks

Don't try to surround the center directly.

This principle should be clear to anyone who has played go for a while. Consider the following diagram.

Figure 1. In this admittedly artificial position, white's territory looks far larger than black's. But if we count, we find that white has only 121 points while black has 136! The thing to remember is that an area in the center tends to look larger than it actually is.

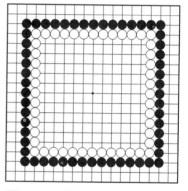

Another reason for not going directly after a large center area is that it is likely to be open on one or more sides and very easy to reduce, while your opponent has probably made a lot of secure territory on the sides.

Figure 1. White's territory only *looks* bigger.

This proverb shouldn't be followed blindly, however. What it warns against is giving away a lot of secure territory for one *huge* moyo (a large framework of potential territory). Indirectly building up a moyo is, in fact, a powerful way to play and can be extremely effective. The concept of moyo is a fundamental pillar of go theory, and there is absolutely nothing wrong in playing a moyo game.

But there is a danger in thinking that a moyo is all yours and trying to take it all or starting an all-or-nothing fight against a modest reducing move. You *want* your opponent to invade so you can turn it into a reasonable amount of secure territory while attacking the invaders. If instead your opponent makes a light reduction of your moyo, simply defend and take points that way.

Reduce a moyo gently with a shoulder hit or a capping play.

This proverb gives you two ways to reduce an opponent's moyo, or large framework of potential territory. When it seems likely that your opponent will enlarge his sphere of influence at the first opportunity, you must act quickly to frustrate his intentions.

In dealing with a moyo, you have two choices: a deep invasion, hoping to lay waste to the whole area, or a more modest erasing move such as a shoulder hit or a capping play. Let's compare the two approaches.

Some players automatically invade their opponents' positions even though the defender can blockade the invader using a shoulder hit or a capping play (Figure 2), but this sort of vandalism is easily punished.

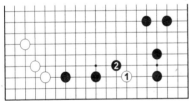

Figure 2. Example 1 – an invasion is a bad idea.

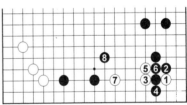

Figure 3. A little better, but. . . .

Figure 2. To prevent the black moyo from becoming even larger, white unthinkingly invaded with 1. Black immediately played the shoulder hit of 2, a painful attack in every respect. Clearly, trying to destroy the whole area with a deep invasion was a mistake. With no guarantee of living, white's haste has doomed his game to utter ruin with a single stroke.

Figure 3. White's sequence through 7 is a little better, but black 8 makes this result quite unfavorable as well. Any thought of a deep invasion is likely to be a bad idea unless it is carefully read out beforehand.

Figure 4. The shoulder hit is perfect for this situation. White doesn't need to worry about an assault at **A**, as he can simply reply with **B**.

Black's only choices in this position are **B** and **C**.

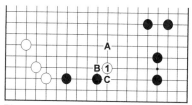

Figure 4. Try the shoulder hit instead.

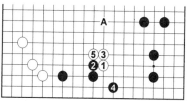

Figure 5. Pushing up first.

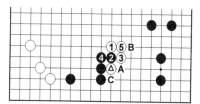

Figure 6. White's second option.

Figure 5. In the first variation, black first pushes up to provoke 3. Because of the shoulder hit, white is one step ahead in the chase out into the center. Black can only strengthen white by pushing again, so a slide to 4 takes a little profit and deprives white of a base for his stones. Playing at 5 next, or more lightly at **A**, settles the white stones for the moment.

Figure 6. The one-space jump of 1 is a lighter move than the stretch of the last figure and moves out faster. Black wedges in with 2 and, after the atari and connection, white 5 settles the position. Note that connecting at **A** would be a bad mistake – a black cut at 5 would be severe, and trying to save the marked stone is small anyway.

Instead of pushing through with 2, black may well attach at **A**. White must not fight a losing battle by dropping down to **C**, but instead play **B** to settle the important stones first.

Figure 7. Black can also respond to the shoulder hit by pushing along the side with 1. White will respond with 2, though there is also the one-space jump at **B**, which aims at the peep at **A** later. (Don't even think of playing 2 at **C**.) Black continues with the keima of 3 and white settles the position with 4.

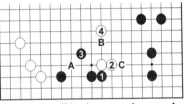

Figure 7. Black can also push sideways.

Figure 8. Instead of the knight's move, black can turn as shown here. White jumps to 2, black peeps at **A** with 3, then white plays lightly at 4. (Allowing white to play at 3 gives his stones excellent shape and effectively ends any chance of attack black may have had on this group.) White is not concerned with the

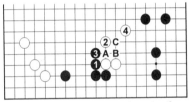

Figure 8. An alternative to the knight's move.

stones at the bottom – if black cuts at **C**, white plays atari from the top and sacrifices them to gain sente to play a big point somewhere else.

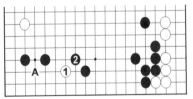

Figure 9. Example 2: an invasion.

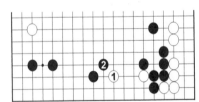

Figure 10. Example 3: this is even worse.

Figure 9. Here's another example. White has felt it necessary to invade at 1. Aided by the peep at **A**, he may live in this space but the result would be disastrous in this position – black will seal white in, building overwhelming thickness and threatening the stone on the left. White has neglected whole-board thinking to take immediate profit and will pay dearly for it.

Figure 10. This invasion is even worse than the first. The attack of black 2 is distressing – it is mindless to burden yourself with weak stones that you have to defend this early in the game. There is a good alternative to these two foolhardy invasions, though – the capping move.

Figure 11. When white 1 caps the black stone, it is natural for black to take profit with 2. White 3, skipping lightly out into the center, can be a great move if the situation at the top of the board warrants it.

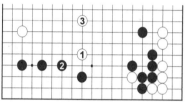

Figure 11. The capping play is ideal here.

Figure 12. If black dodges to the other side, white can forego **A** and play the excellent combination of 2 and 4. White also has the attachment of **B** for later. The lesson is: Don't try to make territory from thickness directly.

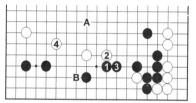

Figure 12. The other knight's move is not good.

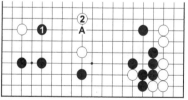

Figure 13. Black's counter to the capping play.

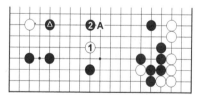

Figure 14. White 1 starts an impossible fight.

Figure 13. Besides the two knight's moves we discussed, black has the "sideways" counter of 1. White has to take this opportunity to escape with 2 – answering the distraction of 1 would give black two groups to attack. White can't allow black to cap him in turn, not with the stone at 1 lying in wait. Note that jumping to **A** is not fast enough.

Figure 14 (last page). A word of warning – don't apply the capping move automatically. In this figure, black has already played the marked stone and his moyo has become very deep. If white unthinkingly plays 1, black will cap him in turn and the fight will become almost hopeless. White **A** is the correct way to reduce the black framework here.

Erase big frameworks shallowly.

For one reason or another, your opponent's moyo may become so deep that a shoulder hit or capping play would come under immediate attack. Instead of simply reducing the moyo, the stone would find itself running for its life, helping the opponent to convert much of the moyo into solid, unassailable territory. In such cases, it might be best to drop a stone just inside the enemy lines in a sort of "paratrooper" invasion.

Figure 15. Here's a good example of such a by-the-seat-of-the-pants invasion. It is taken from a professional game. Keeping in mind the possibility of a jump to **A**, black has found just the point to reduce the moyo with 1. If white plays **B**, black **C** naturally flows into the moyo from the other direction and maintains a nice balance. Going any further into the moyo than this would be a big mistake.

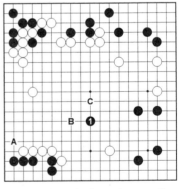

Figure 15. A "paratrooper" attack.

Make the horse's face or the giraffe's neck to enlarge your moyo.

Figure 16. Black 1, a large knight's move from the two marked stones, is a common way to enlarge your moyo. The shape formed is known as the "horse's face." This move requires careful timing, since white would also like to play in this area to fix up his moyo at the bottom of the board.

Black 3 again hits the point that both sides want to occupy after the 1 – 2 exchange. With these two moves, black has established quite a large moyo that white will have to approach with care.

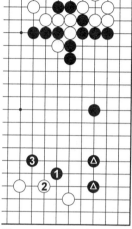

Figure 16. The horse's face.

Figure 17. Black can extend one space more as shown. This move and the marked stones form the shape known as the "giraffe's neck," yet another popular way to enlarge a moyo.

Black plays 3 and 5 because the connection between 1 and the marked stones is rather weak.

White may not play 2, however. A common reply to 1 is white **A**, black **B**, followed by a white reinforcement at **C**.

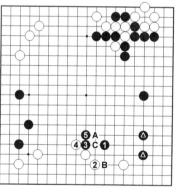

Figure 17. The giraffe's neck formation.

Approaching a loose invasion.

Often when you're building a moyo your opponent will make a loose invasion that allows him a two-space extension to either side. While the proverb says not to rush to play on a miai point, sooner or later the game will dictate that you approach from one direction or the other.

The question is which side should you approach from? This can be a thorny problem.

Figure 18. White 1 is what we call a loose invasion, and white will defend his stone by extending to either **A** or **B**, depending on black's next move in this area.

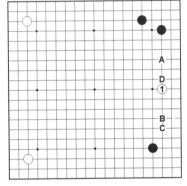

Figure 18. A loose invasion.

If black chooses to approach from his shimari, white can simply defend by extending to **B**. Given black's hoshi stone at the bottom, though, white is probably better off by making his own approach move at **C**. But this may be just a matter of taste.

Or black may approach from his hoshi stone at **B**, in which case, white should extend to **A**.

By the way, white chose to invade at 1 instead of approaching at **C** to prevent a black pincer that would work well with the shimari in the upper right corner. That is another acceptable way of playing but would lead to a different sort of game. White can also play 1 at **D**.

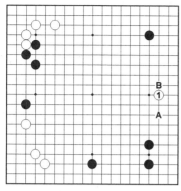

Figure 19. Here's another loose invasion where white can gain safety by extending two spaces to either side. (He can also play a keima against the star point on this side.)

In this case, black has a one-space enclosure with an open skirt, facing an extension on the lower side. In this position, he should extend to **A** to more or less close this corner off (white still has reducing moves against this structure).

Figure 19. The perfect invasion.

Note that playing **B** would be bad for white because it would give black a bigger corner. Even though a white invasion here would be easier, black may well get to this area first and solidify a larger territory.

Chapter 7
Life and Death

There is death in the hane.

When you feel that you can kill an enemy group, there are two things to look for: the best way to narrow the group's eye space, and the vital point of the position. The hane, a diagonal move around an enemy stone, is a common technique.

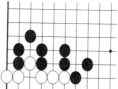

Figure 1. Black to kill.

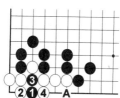

Figure 2. First try.

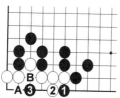

Figure 3. Try the hane.

Figure 1. Black is to play and kill. The proverb gives you a big hint, but what variations are likely to follow?

Figure 2. First, if black tries playing in the middle of the group, white responds with 2 which forces 3 and 4. Now black has to play at both 3 and **A** in order to kill, so white is alive.

Figure 3. Black 1 is the hane that kills. If white 2, black 3 takes out an eye (**A** and **B** are called miai – if white takes one, black takes the other).

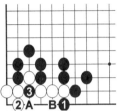

Figure 4. The hane works: white is dead.

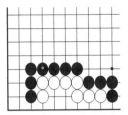

Figure 5. Try to kill white.

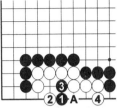

Figure 6. This won't work.

Figure 4. White might respond to 1 by making an eye immediately, but this doesn't work either – after black plays 3, **A** and **B** are miai and the white group is dead..

Figure 5. Black to play and kill. Which hane works? Or do they both do the job?

Figure 6. Let's see what playing inside does first. Black 1 looks like the key point for making two eyes but white plays 2, which forces 3, and white 4 widens the eye space enough to let him live. If black plays **A**, the result is seki: this is an end game move.

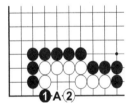

Figure 7. This hane doesn't work.

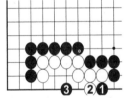

Figure 8. Success!

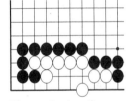

Figure 9. Another example: kill white.

Figure 7. The hane at the left doesn't work, as white takes the vital point for life with 2 (white can also play at **A** and live).

Figure 8. The hane at the right is the correct answer. Blocking at 2 only invites a strike at the vital point of 3.

Figure 9. Here's a classic life-and-death problem: black to play and kill. It's a little harder than the others – if you don't see the answer quickly, you probably won't find it.

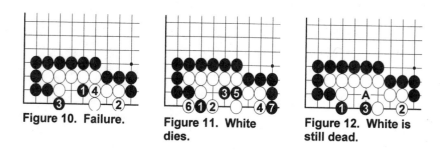

Figure 10. Failure.   Figure 11. White dies.   Figure 12. White is still dead.

Figure 10. Again, we'll look at the "obvious" move first. Poking at what appears to be a vital point with 1 forces white to make an eye with 2. The hane threatens to connect, but white 4 still captures black 1 because of shortage of liberties and the group is alive.

Figure 11. The hane on the left is the move to kill. If white plays 2 to make this an eye, 3 is forced. White makes what he hopes will be a second eye at 4, but black 5 puts the six white stones in atari and 7 captures the three white stones on the right.

Figure 12. So what happens if white makes his eye on the other side? In this case, black just jumps to 3 (not **A** – this would revert to the position in Figure 10 where white is alive). Now white's second eye is false, and white is caught in a shortage of liberties after the throw-in between 1 and 3. White is nicely dead.

There is life in the hane.

Figure 13. This life-and-death proverb is the companion to the first one and demonstrates the effectiveness of the simple hane in handling tactical problems. Black to play, using the presence of the marked hane stone to live.

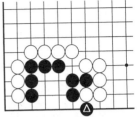

Figure 13. Black to play.

Figure 14. Black 1 is a great move – it is not obvious but it is very effective. After the sequence shown, white can not connect to take away the eye at the bottom, so black is alive. Superb!

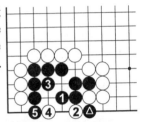

Figure 14. White can't connect!

Play at the center of symmetry.

Symmetrical positions occur often in actual play. In many cases, the vital point is right at the center of the structure.

Figure 15. Black is completely surrounded and has to make two eyes – there is no way to escape or kill white. There are three points of interest at the center of the group for black to consider. Which one would you play?

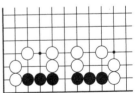

Figure 15. Black to play.

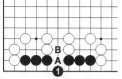

Figure 16. Black 1 is the kosumi.

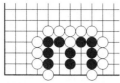

Figure 17. Black to live.

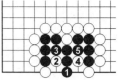

Figure 18. Alive!

Figure 16. Black's kosumi of 1 gives him one eye on each side.

Figure 17. Black to play. This should be easy for you.

Figure 18. Black 1 is the key. White has nothing after this.

The comb formation is alive.

Figure 19. The white stones in the figure make what is known as the comb formation, which is alive as it stands. If black plays **A**, white responds with **B** and vice-versa.

Of course, if the white stones are completely surrounded, black can kill with **B** because each two-stone leg would have a shortage of liberties.

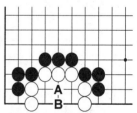

Figure 19. The comb formation is alive.

The rabbity six is dead.

The rabbity six is the largest space that can be reduced to one eye. It does, however, take twelve moves to fill its inside liberties (see "3 = 3, 4 = 5, 5 = 8, 6 = 12").

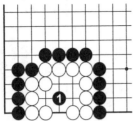

Figure 20. The rabbity six.

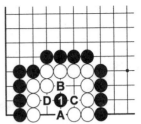

Figure 21. A bigger eye space is alive.

Figure 20. This group has a rabbity-six eye space – the side that gets to play at 1 determines whether it lives or dies.

Figure 21. This is not a rabbity-six group, since it has seven spaces inside. Black 1 seems to strike at the vital point, but white **A**, then **B**, **C**, and **D** ensure that the group is alive in seki.

Six die and eight live.

This proverb applies to stones on the second line and is helpful when deciding how far to crawl before switching somewhere else.

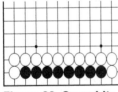

Figure 22. Can white kill?

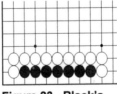

Figure 23. Black's status now?

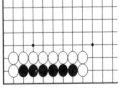

Figure 24. Can black still live?

Figures 22 – 24. In each problem, read out what will happen if white plays first and if black plays first.

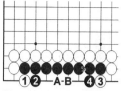 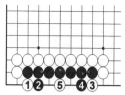 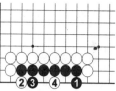

| Figure 25. Black is alive no matter what. | Figure 26. White can kill if it's his turn. | Figure 27. No way for black to live. |

Figure 25. The eight-stone black group is alive unconditionally. Even after white plays two hanes, **A** and **B** are miai to live.

Figure 26. The seven-stone black group is unsettled. If white plays first, he can hane twice then make black's eye space into one big eye with 5 and thus kill the group. If it is black's turn, he can live by playing at either 1 or 3.

Figure 27. Black should save the five-space group for ko threats and play somewhere else – his group is dead, even if he plays first.

In the corner, four die and six live.

This proverb also applies to stones on the second line. It can help simplify a complicated situation quickly.

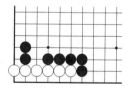 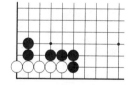 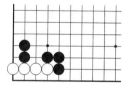

| Figure 28. What is white's status? | Figure 29. And this group's? | Figure 30. Can white live? |

Figures 28 – 30. Take black and try to kill each of these second-line corner positions.

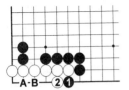

Figure 31. White is alive no matter what happens.

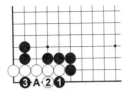

Figure 32. The five-stone corner group is unsettled.

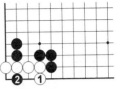

Figure 33. The four-stone group is un-conditionally dead.

Figure 31. The six-stone corner group is unconditionally alive. The best black can do is the hane of 1, but white blocks with 2 and lives because **A** and **B** are miai.

Figure 32. The five-stone group in the corner is unsettled. If it is black's turn, he can kill the group with the hane of 1 then the placement of 3. If it is white's turn, though, he lives by playing at 1 himself.

Figure 33. The correct answer is for black to do nothing. The four-stone corner group is dead no matter what – even if it is white's turn, there is no hope.

On the third line, four die and six live.

Not surprisingly, it's easier to make life on the third line than on the second (where "six die, eight live").

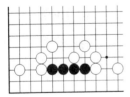

Figure 34. Black can't live.

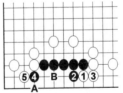

Figure 35. The un-settled case.

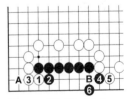

Figure 36. Black is completely alive.

Figure 34. Black has four stones on the third line, and they are dead. As an exercise, take black and try to live.

Figure 35. Five stones on the third line live or die according to whose turn it is. If it is white's turn, he will hane and connect to kill the black group. If black **A**, white **B** finishes off the group.

Figure 36. With six stones on the third line, the group is alive as it stands. Even if white plays hane and connects, black can live by playing a hane himself with 4.

Some care must be taken in applying this proverb, however. If, for example, white has a stone at **A**, then he need not connect at 3 but can hane at **B** instead and kill black.

The rectangular six is alive.

This proverb tells us that the two-by-three eye space is alive, as long as there is no bad aji. There are variations of the six-point eye space (such as the "comb" group, the "rabbity six," and various corner positions), but these have to be studied on their own – even though they look alike, they can be quite different according to the number and location of liberties, "legs," and the peculiarities of the corner.

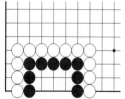 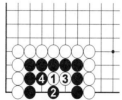 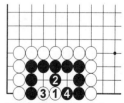

Figure 37. The rectangular six is alive.

Figure 38. There's not even bad aji.

Figure 39. The other invasion fails, too.

Figure 37. This is the basic rectangular six. There are no weaknesses and the shape is alive as it stands. Note that the black stones have to be connected, or it may be possible to kill the group. This also applies to the door group, for which the eye space is two spaces on the edge and three high.

Figures 38 and 39 (last page). To have any chance of killing the black group, white has to invade and try to make the inside points into one big eye somehow. As we see here, there is no possibility of doing this and black is unconditionally alive.

In the corner, the rectangular six needs outside liberties to live.

Although the rectangular six on the side is alive, the same shape in the corner needs outside liberties to survive.

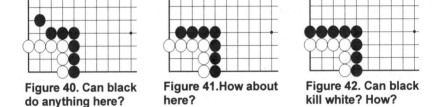

Figure 40. Can black do anything here?

Figure 41.How about here?

Figure 42. Can black kill white? How?

Figure 40. Can black kill the corner, even by ko?

Figure 41. Black to play again. What happens?

Figure 42. White has no outside liberties. What's black's best move?

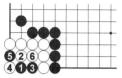

Figure 43. Example
1: White lives.

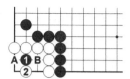

Figure 44. White is
still alive.

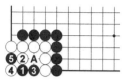

Figure 45. Example
2: Result is ko.

Figure 43. Black really has only the 1–2 and 2–2 points to consider. This sequence is forced if black wants to have any chance of killing white, but white turns out to be alive anyway.

Figure 44. The placement of 1 at the 2–2 point doesn't go anywhere either. After the attachment of 2, **A** and **B** are miai.

Figure 45. When there is only one outside liberty, black 1 is the vital point and the sequence of Figure 43 doesn't work any more because white is now the one who is short of liberties. The result is ko.

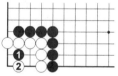

Figure 46. Black 1
lets white live.

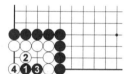

Figure 47. Example
3: black 1 leads to a
ko.

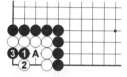

Figure 48. Black 1
kills white.

Figure 46. The 2–2 placement of 1 doesn't work. White lives easily.

Figure 47. When there are no outside liberties at all, the situation is different. Playing 1 at the 1–2 point gives a ko, but there is a better move.

Figure 48. Now playing 1 at the 2–2 point kills the white group. White can't play at **A** because he is short of liberties.

Bent four in the corner is dead.

This proverb is part of the official rules of most national go associations.

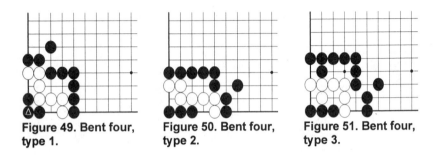

Figure 49. Bent four, type 1.

Figure 50. Bent four, type 2.

Figure 51. Bent four, type 3.

Figures 49 – 51. There are three types of bent-four shapes in the corner, and they are all dead.

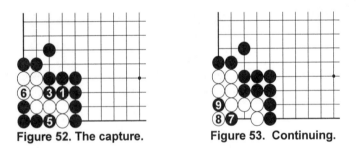

Figure 52. The capture.

Figure 53. Continuing.

Figure 52. Let's take a look at the first example and see why this position is considered dead.

To begin with, white can't play anywhere inside without killing himself (after filling the outside liberties, black forces white to take the three stones, then plays at the 1–1 point, making one eye).

If black claims that white is dead, his only way to prove it would start with the atari of 5, which forces white to capture.

Figure 53. Continuing, black plays 7. White must play 8 to start a ko, otherwise a black play there kills white. Black of course takes the ko but, at the absolute end of the game, there are very few ko threats left (if any).

If all this were necessary, black could spend a few points to nullify the ko threats then begin the sequence shown here. However, the bent-four rule was instituted to avoid all this, so it is not necessary to play out the sequence to kill the corner.

You must know ko to understand the carpenter's square.

If you understand the carpenter's square, you must be a six dan.

The three-by-three eye space in the corner is called the carpenter's square and it is one of the toughest life-and-death positions. Usually, a big ko fight can be started to kill the corner, although there are often quite a few ways to do so.

The original version of the second proverb was "If you understand the carpenter's square, you must be shodan," but this was before the recent dan inflation. The shodan (1d) of those days more nearly corresponds to six dan today.

Even so, a modern shodan has begun to incorporate basic ko strategies in his play and will benefit from a careful study of the carpenter's square. Five stones' worth of study should get the basic patterns down pat. . . .

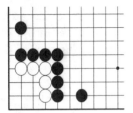

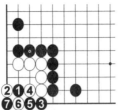

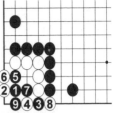

Figure 54. The carpenter's square.

Figure 55. Variation 1: ko.

Figure 56. White 4 is a mistake.

Figure 54. This figure shows the basic carpenter's square. It has no liberties on the outside. Where should black invade?

Figure 55. Black 1 is the only move. Likewise, white has to answer at 2 and, if black plays hane, the situation becomes ko as shown. (By the way, the answer diagrams for this problem also apply to the case when the white group has one liberty on the outside.)

Figure 56. White can't block directly in the last figure, as black continues as shown and converts white's space into a single big eye. White is dead.

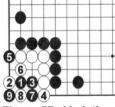

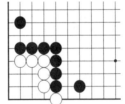

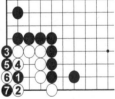

Figure 57. Variation 2: ko.

Figure 58. Another example.

Figure 59. Another ko.

Figure 57. Instead of the hane in Figure 55, black can simply extend with 3. If white lets black connect, the white group has only one big eye. Unfortunately, white has to find the first ko threat.

Figures 58 and 59. Here's another example. White has added a hane, expecting to improve the group's chances at life. Surprisingly, white's hane hasn't strengthened his corner at all. The standard sequence follows as shown: ko again!

Figure 60. Here's one last example. This is called the weak carpenter's square because the 4–4 point is open and the white stones are much weaker than before. What happens if black plays first?

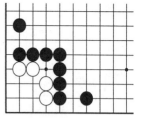

Figure 60. A slightly different position.

Figure 61. Because the corner of the square is missing, white is dead if black moves first. Black can also play 3 at 9 (white 4 at 6 is about the best answer, but black plays to the right of 4 and white is dead again).

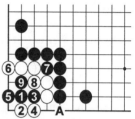

White can live by playing at 1 before black (this is true for all the positions we looked at). A white hane at **A** isn't enough, although he can live with ko.

Figure 61. White is dead.

Strange things happen at the 1–2 point.

The corner in a go game is a strange and magical place – the most amazing moves seem to come out of nowhere, as anyone who takes black in high-handicap games can attest.

These wild and wonderful combinations in the corner seem to center on the 1–2 point, which is pivotal to many corner positions.

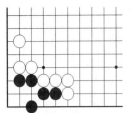

Figure 62. White to play.

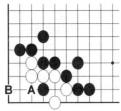

Figure 63. White to live.

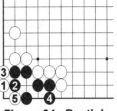

Figure 64. Death by ko.

Figure 62. White to play. You can kill black by ko if you find the right sequence.

Figure 63. White to play again. This is the same idea, but this time we want to make the corner live. (White **A** doesn't work because of black **B**.)

Figure 64. The placement of white 1 at the 1–2 point is the correct answer to the problem in Figure 62 and takes the vital point of the black group's shape. Living with ko is the best that black can do.

Playing 1 at 2 instead doesn't work because black plays at 1, making the points 4 and 5 miai – if white takes one, black takes the other and lives.

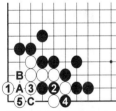

Figure 65. White is alive!

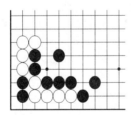

Figure 66. Black to play.

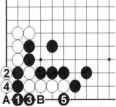

Figure 67. The 1–2 point is the key!

Figure 65. The 1–2 point is the key to this problem too, but this time it gives life, rather than taking it away. Black 2 and 4 take a little profit, but then the other 1–2 point gives life to the rest of the white stones.

If black plays 2 at 3, then white 2, black **A**, white **B**, black 5, and white **C** gives a bigger life.

Figure 66 This time it is black's turn to play. Black's two stones have three liberties and white's have four, so black needs a clever move.

Figure 67. Dropping down to the 1–2 point is the key to this position. Now the liberties are four to four, and black wins the race to capture since white can't play at **A** or **B** because of a shortage of liberties.

But what if black panics and tries to take away one of white's liberties by playing a hane at 3 instead of 1? In that case, white first plays at the vital 1–2 point (atari), black takes, and white plays **B** to start a ko. This is a shame.

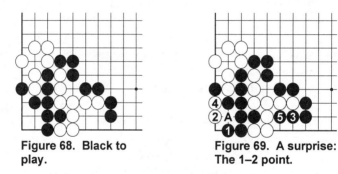

Figure 68. Black to play.

Figure 69. A surprise: The 1–2 point.

Figure 68. Black to play. Black has eight stones, white nine. Each can make an eye if given the chance. How will this turn out?

Figure 69. Just follow the proverb and play at the 1–2 point. Moves 1 to 5 follow, and white can't atari at **A** because he is short of liberties.

Black can't play 1 at 3 to reduce white's liberties in a straightforward race to capture, because white himself will play at the 1–2 point and win. Playing at 2 instead of 1 doesn't work either – white plays at 1, and the position becomes ko.

Maeda Nubuaki, 9-dan (1907 – 1975) documented his exhaustive studies of life and death in the corner and wrote many books on the subject. Here is one of his most famous problems:

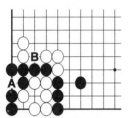

Figure 70. Black to play.

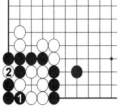

Figure 71. Huh?

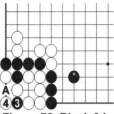

Figure 72. Black 3 is atari and sets up ko.

Figure 70. Black to play. This is a classic go problem in life and death. The straightforward connection at **A** fails because white will play **B** so black can't atari.

Figures 71 and 72. Black 1 is a counterintuitive move, but it works. This is a famous eye-stealing tesuji. After white takes at 2, black throws in at 3 (atari). Playing at **A** instead loses.

Figure 73. At this point, black just takes the ko. White can't connect, so he has to find a ko threat somewhere else. Black will have to ignore two ko threats to finally capture the stones, but this is still a good result considering how far behind he was to begin with.

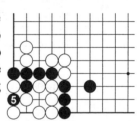

Figure 73. Now comes the ko!

All four-space eyes are alive except the square four.

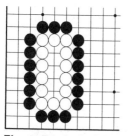

Figure 74. A straight four eye space is alive.

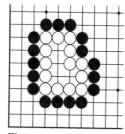

Figure 75. The L-4 eye space is also safe.

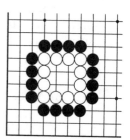

Figure 76. But a square four eye space is dead.

Figures 74 and 75. The straight four and L-4 eye spaces can be made into two independent eyes if attacked.

Figure 76. The square four is the only eye space of this type that is dead.

Enlarge eye space to live.
Reduce eye space to kill.

These are perhaps the most basic life-and-death proverbs. They apply in most cases, except when there is a vital point.

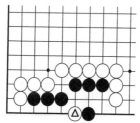

Figure 77. Try to make the black group live.

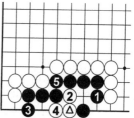

Figure 78. The answer is to enlarge the eye space.

Figure 77 (last page). Black to play and live by applying the proverb. White has played the marked stone to try to convert the black group's eye space into one big eye.

Figure 78 (last page). Black 1 is just the move. If white wants to continue to prevent black from making two eyes, he has to play 2 and answer 3 with 4. But now, black connects at 5 and lives in seki.

Play at the vital point to kill.

A careful examination of the opponent's eye space may reveal a placement within the enemy camp that will kill. You can often kill a group by playing at the same vital point that your opponent needs to occupy to live.

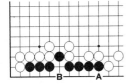

Figure 79. White to kill.

Figure 80. First try.

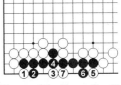

Figure 81. Hane first!

Figure 79. White to play and kill. White **A** doesn't work because of black **B**.

Figure 80. White 1 is the right idea but the wrong timing. Black simply connects and has eight stones on the second line which, the proverb tells us, are alive. (White can play **A** and make a seki, but this is end-game play.)

Figure 81. White must first hane with 1 then, after black defends, he can make the placement of 3 that will kill the black group as shown. By the way, if black plays 2 at 5 to forestall a white hane there, white will play at 2 himself and, if black blocks, white at 4 finishes the group.

Chapter 8
Running, Connecting, and Capturing

Escape lightly with the large knight's move.

When your stones come under attack, escape becomes imperative if they can not make easy life. In order of speed, popular escaping moves include the diagonal move (kosumi), one-point jump (ikken tobi), knight's move (keima), two-space jump (nikken tobi), and large knight's move (ogeima).

When choosing among these, you must balance how quickly each moves into the center against the thinness of the move (its susceptibility to cuts, peeps, and other plays that the opponent may use against the fleeing stones).

When escaping from a particularly strong enemy position, the large knight's move is a valuable technique. Just remember that this move is light and fast but can be cut. Check that you can sacrifice a stone or two, preferably with sente, before using it to run away.

Chase with the knight's move, but escape with the one-point jump.

When chasing a group or running away with one of your own, speed and strength are vital. The one-point jump and the knight's move – although they can be cut, the connection with the advancing stone is not as weak as with the two-space jump or the large knight's move and your opponent is much less likely to cut immediately. You should look for forcing moves to play later that will cover any cuts that may arise.

When an immediate cut isn't profitable, the one-point jump is an ideal escape technique – it is pretty much the standard move. And when going after your opponent's stones, chase them with the knight's move – it has the advantage of leaning into the enemy stones and restricting their movement, as well as jumping ahead quickly.

Jump down to the first line to connect.

If it looks as though your group is about to be captured, consider your opponent's position. If it is open at the bottom, there may be a connection for you on the first line. If so, you may be treated to a great wailing and gnashing of teeth when you play there and save your stones.

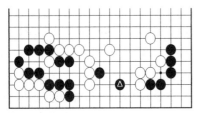

Figure 1. Can you find black's connection?

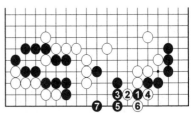

Figure 2. One idea.

Figure 1. This position appeared in a recent game. There's a clever technique here to connect the drifting black stones (it involves moving with the marked stone down to the first line), but the connection was overlooked. Can you find the magic move?

Figure 2. Here's one possibility – black first plays a hane at 1 to put the plan into motion. Moves 2 through 4 follow naturally, but black 5 is a surprise! White has to capture with 6 to prevent this connection, but then black jumps along the first line and connects to the left.

Unfortunately, black has lost a lot of points in the corner. Can he do better?

Figure 3. Black can play the clever combination of 1 and 3 to connect. This is much better, but black hasn't made any real profit. Considering the various weaknesses of the white corner, can you find an even better sequence?

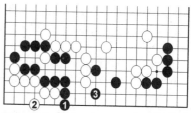

Figure 3. The second idea.

Figure 4. How about applying the technique of Figure 2 to the left side? Again, dropping down to the first line is the key. If white is careless and grabs the black stone, black will play 7 and 9 and kill the corner.

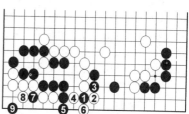

Figure 4. The best solution.

The kosumi connection is not always good.

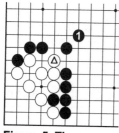

Figure 5. The ever-popular kosumi.

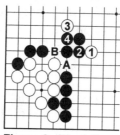

Figure 6. Black 2 and 4 make bad shape.

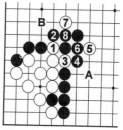

Figure 7. More bad shape.

Figure 5. Among amateur players, the kosumi connection of 1 is a popular response to the double peep of the marked white stone because it protects against both cutting points at one time. This connection should not be used except in an emergency.

Figure 6 (last page). The reason why you should avoid connecting with the kosumi is that it is vulnerable to peeps. Here, black has been forced to make a four-stone dumpling in answer to the peeps of white 1 and 3. (Answering 1 and 3 at **A** and **B** would have been better, but the black stone at the diagonal becomes a wasted move.)

Figure 7 (last page). White may well push first before peeping at 5 and 7 here. This gives additional forcing moves at **A** and **B**.

Figure 8. A solid connection at 1 or 2 is correct. White can push through and cut, but it's hard to see how that can be at all useful. The only thing white has accomplished in this figure is to force black to strengthen his position and make white 4 a target for attack.

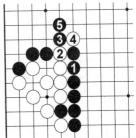

Figure 8. The correct answer.

This finishes our coverage of the proverbs dealing with chasing enemy stones, running away, and connecting to friendly forces. The remainder of the chapter will concentrate on the methods for winning a race to capture.

In a race to capture, or semeai, the players each have a group that is penned in, cannot make two eyes, and shares common liberties with the enemy group. The fate of a group in a semeai depends on whether it has an eye, how many and what type of liberties it has, and whether any approach moves need to be made.

The rest of the proverbs in this chapter will help you simplify complex positions and to avoid the more common mistakes.

Cut to gain a liberty.

Figure 9. White is ready to play on the 1–1 point and atari the black stones. Black is clearly behind in the semeai, or race to capture, so he has to do something clever to have any chance of survival.

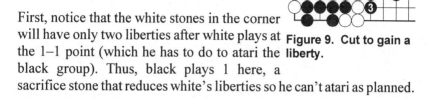

First, notice that the white stones in the corner will have only two liberties after white plays at the 1–1 point (which he has to do to atari the black group). Thus, black plays 1 here, a sacrifice stone that reduces white's liberties so he can't atari as planned.

Figure 9. Cut to gain a liberty.

This stone has two liberties that must be occupied before white can play in the corner, which gives black the chance to continue playing on the outside and win the fight.

Fill outside liberties first.

Let's start by defining terms. There are three types of liberties in a semeai: an outside liberty is a liberty that one group has but the other does not; a shared liberty is one that is common to both groups; and an internal liberty is one inside an eye.

In most semeais, you should start by filling outside liberties first. When these are filled, continue with the internal ones. Fill shared liberties last. Outside liberties affect only the opponent's group. So do internal liberties but, if you misread the semeai, you lose one point each time your opponent fails to answer. The last ones to be filled are the shared liberties because they reduce the liberties of both groups.

Be sure to start a semeai by filling your opponent's outside liberties. This is perhaps the most important rule for fighting a race to capture.

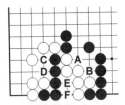

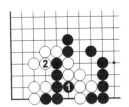

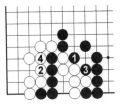

Figure 10. Types of liberties in a race to capture.

Figure 11. A quick death.

Figure 12. The correct answer.

Figure 10. Black to play. White's two outside liberties are **A** and **B**, black's are **C** and **D**, and the two groups share **E** and **F**.

Figure 11. Black 1 fills a shared liberty, and his group dies almost immediately.

Figure 12. This black 1 fills one of white's outside liberties and is the correct answer. The result is a seki, where both groups live.

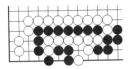

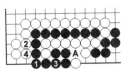

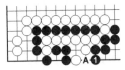

Figure 13. Black to play.

Figure 14. Short on liberties.

Figure 15. The correct answer.

Figure 13. Here is another problem with black to play again.

Figure 14. With 1, black fills in one of his own liberties. Now he can't play **A** to atari the white group.

Figure 15. This is the right answer. Black has to make an approach move before he can fill in any of white's outside liberties. No matter what white does next, black will play **A** next and win the race to capture.

In a race to capture, take the ko last.

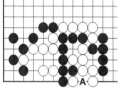

Figure 16. Black to play.

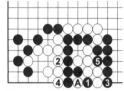

Figure 17. White 6 at A.

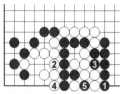

Figure 18. The correct answer.

Figure 16. Black to play. The ko at **A** is the key here.

Figure 17. This is what happens when black starts the fight by capturing the ko. Play continues through black 5, but then white takes the ko and puts the black stones in atari. Now it's up to black to find the first ko threat, a definite disadvantage.

Figure 18. If black leaves the ko until last, their positions are reversed and it is now white who has to find the first ko threat.

One eye beats no eyes.

This proverb describes how, when two groups are trying to kill each other, one with an eye will have a real advantage over another that has none. Consider the following position:

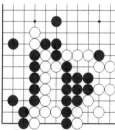

Figure 19. White to live.

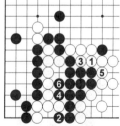

Figure 20. Black gets a seki.

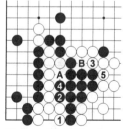

Figure 21. Black loses.

Figure 19 (last page). In this problem, the white stones share four liberties with the attacking black group plus one liberty of their own, for a total of five. Unfortunately, the black group has three outside plus the four shared liberties, for a total of seven.

Figure 20 (last page). If white just starts filling outside liberties (according to the proverb "Fill shared liberties last"), black gets a seki. This is not good enough for white.

Figure 21 (last page). The key to winning the semeai is for white to make an eye first. After the sequence shown, black is clearly doomed. If black plays atari at **A**, white simply captures at **B**.

Sometimes no eye beats one eye.

This is a warning against applying the last proverb then forgetting to keep an eye on the group's outside liberties. Sooner or later, the one-eyed group will have to capture the eyeless stones. There's nothing more annoying than suddenly losing one of your groups as well as some captured stones. Watch out for squeeze plays that can reduce the number of liberties quite quickly.

The larger eye wins the fight.

This saying refers to the fact that large eyes have a sort of "liberty bonus" associated with them that increases with the size of the eye. This occurs because, after the opponent has nearly filled the eye, the attacking stones are captured and the resulting eye has only one fewer liberty than originally (see the next proverb, "3 = 3, 4 = 5, 5 = 8, 6 = 12").

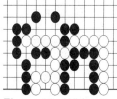

Figure 22. White to play.

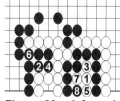

Figure 23. A forced sequence.

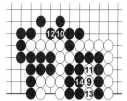

Figure 24. The continuation.

Figure 22. White has allowed his two groups to be cut apart, confident of winning the fight since he has seven liberties, one of which is an eye, and black has only a five-space eye. What's going to happen here?

Figures 23 and 24. White has to start with 1 here to prevent the black group from getting two eyes, and again at 9 for the same reason. Somehow, white has only two liberties now, to black's three. . . .

Figure 25. There's nothing much to be done for white. It would have been better to have left these moves for ko threats later.

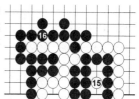

Figure 25. It's all over!

3 = 3, 4 = 5, 5 = 8, and 6 = 12.

This strange-looking proverb helps you remember how many liberties a large eye represents in a semeai: a three-space eye takes three moves to fill; a four-space eye, five; and so on.

Figure 26. To prevent white from making two eyes for his group, black has to start by playing 1 (the sanmoku nakade, which is the first move for filling in a three-space eye). The white group has two more liberties, so a three-space eye clearly provides three liberties in a race to capture.

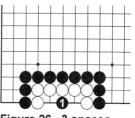

Figure 26. 3 spaces equals 3 liberties.

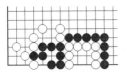

Figure 27. Black to play – can he win?

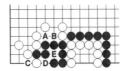

Figure 28. Black's liberties.

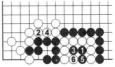

Figure 29. Starting the attack.

Figure 27. This problem illustrates the yomoku nakade (filling in a four-space eye). Black has four liberties to white's four but white's liberties are in one big eye, which the proverb says takes five moves to capture. Can black win if he plays first?

Figure 28. If you noticed that it will take white five moves to capture (**A** through **E**), you have the answer: five moves to five, and since black moves first he will win.

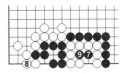

Figure 30. Black wins!

Figures 29 and 30. These two figures finish off the capturing sequence.

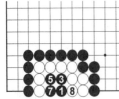

Figure 31. 5 spaces equals 8 liberties.

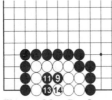

Figure 32. 5 = 8, continued.

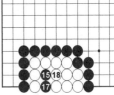

Figure 33. The end.

Figures 31-33. These diagrams illustrate the gomoku nakade, or liberties in a five-space eye (white 2, 4, 6, 10, and 12 are played elsewhere).

These diagrams show that white has gotten six moves somewhere else and has two liberties left. This means that the five-space eye takes a total of eight moves to capture.

Finding the number of liberties for a six-space eye is left to the reader.

Go after the critical stones first.
Set up forcing moves.

When two groups are trying to capture each other, the number of liberties that each has is paramount. The order in which liberties are filled in can also be important, as are the various techniques to force the other side to fill in his own liberties.

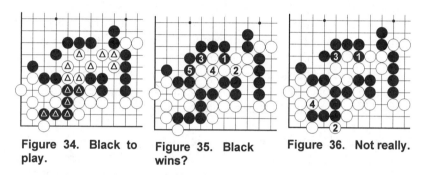

Figure 34. Black to play.

Figure 35. Black wins?

Figure 36. Not really.

Figure 34. Here's a problem to test your skill at capturing. It's black's turn – if the marked black stones are to live, the white stones in the center must die first.

Figure 35. Black 1 is a losing move, but white 2 is also a mistake. These two lapses cancel out and black survives. Can you see how white should play to take advantage of black's shortsightedness?

Figure 36. Instead of 2 in the previous diagram, white should simply start reducing the liberties of the black group. This wins the race to capture. Before going to the next figure, study the position and see if you can figure out why black 1 was bad.

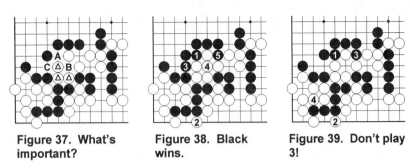

Figure 37. What's important?

Figure 38. Black wins.

Figure 39. Don't play 3!

Figure 37. The first thing to do in a semeai is to determine which stones are important in the fight. Examining this position, we see that what black really has to do is to capture the three marked white stones. The rest of the white stones don't matter except to increase the number of liberties of the marked stones (which they can't in this case). Black's aim here is to occupy the points **A**, **B**, and **C** before white can fill in the three liberties of the endangered black group.

Figure 38. This black 1 is the move to win the semeai. Black 1 sets up the sente atari of 3 on the critical stones at the same time it reduces the white liberties. Black 5 also is a forcing move, and white is clearly dead.

Figure 39. Black 3 is a mistake we hope none of our readers will make. The move does not reduce the liberties of the three vital white stones and gives white the opportunity to redeem the situation.

Chapter 9
Clever Moves,
Forcing Moves, and Sacrifices

Add a stone to the sacrifice on the third line.

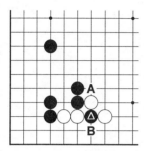

Figure 1. Black to play.

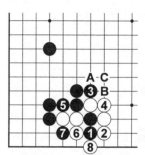

Figure 2. Add another stone.

Figure 1. White has just put the marked stone into atari. The stone can not be saved, but try to find a way to give it up in the most productive manner. (If black plays **A**, white will take the stone and make excellent shape with **B**.)

Figure 2. Adding another stone to the sacrifice is a powerful move – the moves up to 8 are forced, and black gets to build solid central influence and solidify his corner and side. By the way, instead of 3, black can play at 4, then white 3, **A**, **B**, and black **C**.

Add another sacrifice stone to leave aji.

Sacrificing a stone or two can fix up the shape of one of your groups, give it an eye in sente, or make a connection needed to live. The next page shows the classic example of adding an extra sacrifice stone to make solid outside influence.

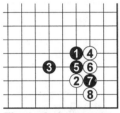

Figure 3. A common 4–5 joseki.

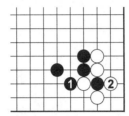

Figure 4. Black 1 is a mistake.

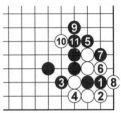

Figure 5. The continuation.

Figure 3. Black plays 1 when he plans to utilize outside influence in his whole-board strategy. What follows is a common joseki that arises from the approach of 2. Black sacrifices a stone at 7 to gain momentum in the follow up.

Figure 4. Black has gained from the sacrifice stone with the atari of 1, but not enough – white can hane at the head of the two black stones and greatly reduce the effectiveness of black's outside influence.

Figure 5. If black increases his sacrifice to two stones, he can close off the right side. Notice that the additional sacrifice doesn't really cost anything: adding an extra stone also adds two liberties to the sacrifice, which white must fill in to capture.

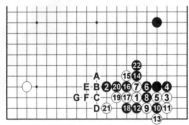

Figure 6. A basic joseki with a lot of aji.

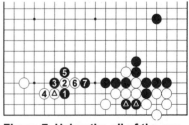

Figure 7. Using the aji of the sacrificed stones.

Figure 6. Here we see a two-space high pincer joseki in the lower right quadrant, quite popular when black has a stone around the middle of the right side. After establishing two sacrifice stones in a critical location, black should probably leave things as they are until the lower left corner is a little clearer.

Black can force white to take the two stones by playing any of **A** to **G**. But these moves are always available, so there is no hurry to play in this area. Similarly, white can start with **C**, black **B**, then **F**, **E**, and **G**, but this gives black a wall of steel in exchange for third-line territory, so it isn't really an option for white right now. This is why neither side is likely to play in the immediate area until later.

Figure 7. If white later makes a shimari with the marked stone, black may well put the aji of the two marked stones into action, starting with the contact play of 1. The crosscut and extension are likely, then black has the beautiful combination of 5 and 7. This puts white in a bind – black 7 occupies point **E** in Figure 6, which you'll recall was sente against the white stones we discussed.

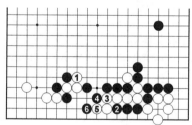

Figure 8. Disaster for white!

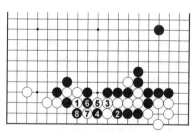

Figure 9. Black captures something.

Figures 8 and 9. Extending up with 1 is a disaster for white – black plays 2 and captures the white group. Coming down with 1 in Figure 9 is also a bad move, as black 7 is a double atari and will capture one of the groups.

Give up worthless stones.

This proverb warns against getting too attached to stones that have served their purpose or to stones that aren't very useful and have no easy way to live or escape. It is important to distinguish these from key stones, such as those separating two weak enemy groups (see the proverb "Don't give up key stones").

Well, how do we decide which stones should be sacrificed? Generally, we include forcing moves (such as the white stones discussed in the figures), ko threats that have been answered, and even overplays.

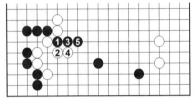

Figure 10. White is unreasonable.   **Figure 11. A clever sacrifice.**

Figure 10. This position results from a common one-space pincer joseki. Black rather precipitously cuts at 1, hoping for exactly the result shown here. For some reason, white cannot bear to part with the four stones, so he tries to rescue them (he should have stopped and asked himself where he was going with them first). Black, on the other hand, is happy to make effortless thickness – if anything happens to the white stones, it's a bonus.

Figure 11. White should have just sacrificed the four stones like this. They have forced black to respond in the corner and have little value any more. In this sequence, white builds a powerful wall with sente then invades at 9. It's hard to see how black can redeem his position after this.

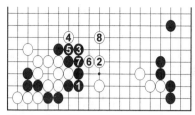

Figure 12. Black 1 is too greedy.

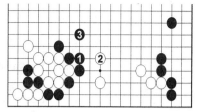

Figure 13. The correct move.

Figure 12. This position also arises from a joseki. Black plays 1 to rescue the stones at the bottom, but a little thought would have shown that there is no time for this right now. White merely jumps with 2 then forces with 4 and 6, then jumps to 8. Black's greed has cursed him with a heavy group of stones that can only be a burden in the running fight to follow.

Figure 13. Black must connect with 1 as shown here. Now that black has a wall in the area, white has to jump with 2 to protect his group.

Figure 14. Black doesn't really have to fear the cut of 2 right now anyway. If white is greedy, black just plays atari twice at 3 and 5 and white's position to the right is precarious indeed.

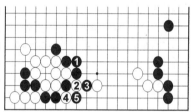

Figure 14. White's greed hurts his position.

Attach at the weasel's belly.

You might think that the two white stones in the corner in the next two figures would have the advantage in the capturing race, but the truth is that their options are severely limited by a shortage of liberties.

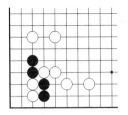

**Figure 15. Example
1 – Black to play.**

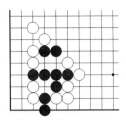

**Figure 16. Example
2 – Black to play.**

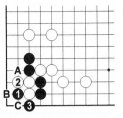

**Figure 17. Black 1 is
the "weasel's belly."**

Figures 15 and 16. Black to play in both cases. The focus of the fight is that each of the black groups in question has three liberties.

Figure 17. An attack on the flank of the white stones (the "weasel's belly") does the trick. Playing at 2 or 3 instead won't do it. If white **B**, black **C** and black still captures the stones.

Figure 18. White 2 is the only answer to black 1, but black 3 next keeps white's liberties down to three. White still can't fill in one of his own liberties at **A**, so black wins easily.

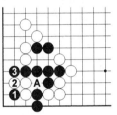

**Figure 18. The same
idea.**

Watch out for a play under the stones.

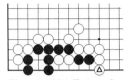

Figure 19. Example 1: black to live.

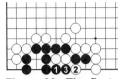

Figure 20. The first try at life.

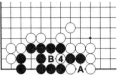

Figure 21. White 4 kills the group.

Figure 19. Here's a problem for you. Can you make black live? Making the black group live looks easy at first glance, but a little reading will show that the answer is not so obvious – pay attention to the marked white stone. The problem here is more one of perception than of reading.

Figure 20. Black 1 here is the first move to consider: straightforward but wrong. Black takes the two white stones but, thanks to white 2, still doesn't have a second eye because of the clever move in the next figure.

Figure 21. The white placement of 4 kills the group. If black captures at **A**, white takes three stones in a snapback; or, if black **B**, white **A**.

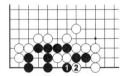

Figure 22. Black is dead here, too.

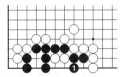

Figure 23. The first move to live.

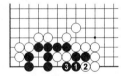

Figure 24. Surprised?

Figure 22. Black can try to take the two white stones the other way, but white throws in with 2 and the continuations revert to the failures already discussed.

Figure 23. Black 1 is the first step in sacrificing the stones on the right to set up the shape that will allow black to play "under the stones." White has to capture these stones to have any chance of killing the black group, but black has an ace up his sleeve!

Figure 24 (last page). White of course plays 2, but then black answers with 3. What's going on here?

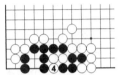

Figure 25. White has to capture.

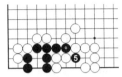

Figure 26. Black lives!

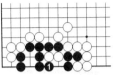

Figure 27. Black 1 is a bad mistake!

Figure 25. White has to capture the four stones, but this loses him one liberty and produces a different shape from the preceding figures.

Figure 26. White's capturing stones are lost when black plays 5, which gives black his second eye. Black plays 5 at one of the points originally occupied by the original black stones, and this is why the sequence is called "playing under the stones."

Figure 27. Black must be careful to atari from the right to force the white stones into a shape that can be captured. This black 1 loses.

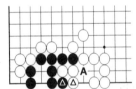

Figure 28. Failure.

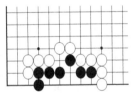

Figure 29. Example 2 – black to live.

Figure 28. This figure shows why the atari by the marked black stone fails. If black plays **A** next, white cannot be captured and just connects to the right.

Figure 29. Here's another problem – black to play and live. There's no way for black to escape into the center, so one of the internal liberties is the key.

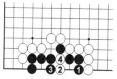

Figure 30. The first step.

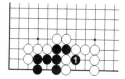

Figure 31. Forced as well.

Figure 32. Black lives!

Figure 30. There is no alternative but for black to maximize the eye space of the group, either on the first line or the third. If we choose 1 as shown here, the remaining moves in this figure are forced.

Figure 31. Black can't connect the stone on the third line, so the moves in this diagram are forced as well.

Figure 32. And now we see that black lives. Playing under the stones is a beautiful combination that most people have trouble seeing in the beginning, but a little practice will help you check for it automatically. You will find this technique a valuable addition to your fighting skills.

Strike at the badger's belly.

This proverb describes a special technique that must be used cautiously, since the nearby stones determine whether it works or not.

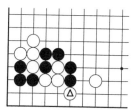

Figure 33. Black to play.

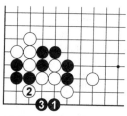

Figure 34. A devilish move.

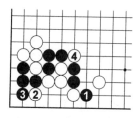

Figure 35. The usual sequence loses.

Figure 33 (last page). White has just played a hane with the marked stone. The common-sense moves won't work, but try reading out the position anyway.

Figure 34 (last page). The surprising move of black 1 is called the badger's belly. If white continues with 2, black 3 is devastating – the three white stones find themselves suddenly short of liberties.

Figure 35 (last page). This black 1 is what is likely to occur to most people first, but it fails because two hanes in effect add one liberty and give white time to cut with 4.

Figure 36. But back to badger. What if white connects at 2 to gain a liberty? Black 3 keeps the pressure on, and white's position folds after black 5.

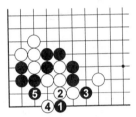

Figure 36. White struggles to no avail.

Beware the two-step hane.

The hane is a simple and effective move, but sometimes following up one hane with another can be devastating because of defects that it introduces in the opponent's shape.

This proverb also warns against applying the two-step (or double) hane automatically because it has a weakness of its own that can make its use questionable in many cases. You should always read out the continuations of this technique, as with any, according to the local position.

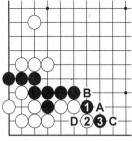

Figure 37. A two-step hane.

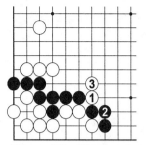

Figure 38. Black gets in trouble.

Figure 37. Black 1 and 3 are the two-step hane and are usually a good combination. White **A**, black **B**, then white **C** doesn't work very well because black **D** is a double atari. Unfortunately, the double hane is dangerous in this case.

Figure 38. In this case, black's eight stones are nearly surrounded on the top and bottom and have no eyes yet. In this case, white will atari and extend as shown to cut black off. Black **D** in the last figure captures a stone to help the small group on the right, but this has no effect on the eight-stone group.

Drop to the second line to set up two hanes.

Figure 39. White 1, 3, and 5 are a great combination for establishing a base in enemy territory. Next, black will block at **A** or **B**, whichever side he thinks is largest, and white will take the other point.

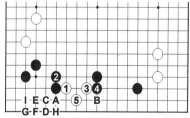

Figure 39. A beautiful combination!

If black plays **B** for example, white will hane at **A** and the sequence black **C**, white **D**, **E**, **F**, **G**, **H**, and **I** follows. White is almost alive and black has lost a lot in these end-game plays. (Jumping out into the center is of major importance at the moment, though.)

Learn the eye-stealing tesuji.

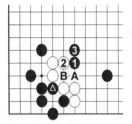

Figure 40. The eye-stealing tesuji.

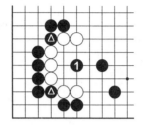

Figure 41. Another vital point to aim for.

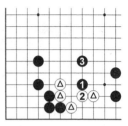

Figure 42. Another fine example.

Figure 40. Black 1 is the vital point in this shape, and white will answer at 2 or **A** (connecting at **B** is very bad, though). Once black reinforces his stone with 3, **B** is very likely to become a false eye for white. The effectiveness of the eye-stealing tesuji usually rests on the presence of friendly stones such as the marked black stone in the figure.

Figure 41. Here, it is the presence of the two marked black stones that makes black 1 so annoying (1 is also at the center of three stones, the topic of another proverb, by the way).

Figure 42. Here, black 1 is the vital point of the marked white stones and reduces white's eye-making capability significantly.

Cut if you can.

This proverb says that cutting your opponent's stones into two groups is usually better than peeping. A peep forces the other side to connect and produces one group that is stronger than either of the two smaller ones.

This saying has to be taken with a grain of salt, however. Most go players pass through a phase in which they cut everything they can, and this just gives the opponent more things to chase after the severed groups are secure. With experience, a sense of balance is acquired that guides the seasoned veteran to the productive cuts and away from overplays.

Don't peep at a cutting point.

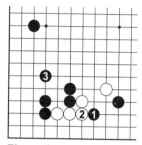

Figure 43. Avoid raw peeps.

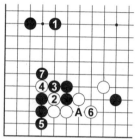

Figure 44. The correct answer.

Figure 43. Black apparently wants to strengthen his stone on the right, so he peeped with 1. Unfortunately, this doesn't really help much and only white is noticeably stronger after the exchange. In addition, black has to go back and play 3 to prevent white from pushing through and cutting.

Figure 44. Black is far better off jumping with 1. Since black 5 threatens the cut of **A**, white has to answer at 6 so black gets the chance to atari the cutting stone with 7. This is the correct way of handling white's combination of push through and cut.

Don't play one atari after another without thinking.

Often you see weak players making one atari after another just for the sake of forcing their opponent to move. This is a bad beginner's habit that must be broken – playing such vulgar moves will only hinder your progress.

Of course this proverb only applies to playing a series of ataris without thinking ahead – you should not hesitate to play an atari when it is called for. Usually a bit of reading will show you how to atari effectively.

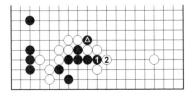

Figure 45. Black to move.

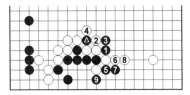

Figure 46. Don't use brute force.

Figure 45. The black stones are in great danger, and the only move that looks good is the push through at 1. If white blocks at 2, how can black best use his marked stone to make life for his group?

Figure 46. A weak player will atari everywhere he can, regardless of the consequences, and will be happy that he has made his group live. But a stronger player will notice that white has been given a huge amount of thickness here at no cost.

Figure 47. It would be better for black to atari from below with 1, rather than using the aji against the three white stones immediately. Playing forcing moves reduces your options, and there's no reason to settle the position right away as in the last diagram.

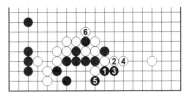

Figure 47. Black 1 is an improvement.

Figure 48. But better yet would be for black to simply cut with 1 here, threatening a double atari. White's best move is the solid connection of 2, which allows black to stretch with 3 and establish a comfortable position. White probably still has to capture the cutting stone with A.

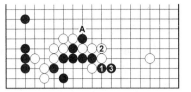

Figure 48. Black 1 is best.

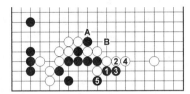

Figure 49. White 2 is a mistake.

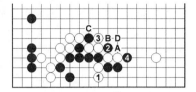

Figure 50. A disaster for white.

Figure 49. What if white extends with 2 instead of connecting? Black continues with 3 and 5 as before and white is left with dangerous aji. Later black at **A** forces white to answer at **B**, and white's group on the left will come under severe attack. This result is clearly inferior to the white positions in Figures 46 through 48.

Figure 50. White might consider dropping down with 1 here, but this doesn't work either. Black simply plays atari with 2 and sets up a ladder with 4 (if white **A**, black **B**, white **C**, then black **D**). This is a disaster for white.

Don't play a forcing move without a reason.

Sometimes deciding whether a forcing move should be played is a problem of exceeding delicacy. A forcing move strengthens the opponent's stones (which can turn out to be very bad later), and it eliminates a ko threat that you may need.

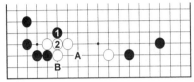

Figure 51. Helping white fix his bad aji.

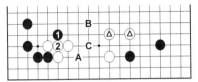

Figure 52. A good forcing move.

Figure 51. Black 1 is the standard example where a forcing move helps the other side. Without the 1 – 2 exchange, black has the invasion at **A** or the large end-game move of **B**, which are no longer nearly as effective as they were before the forcing move.

Figure 52. If white has played the marked stones, the forcing move of 1 is now good because the invasion of **A** is no longer available (assuming that black 1 is useful in the whole-board position). Black may continue with the reducing move of **B**, to which white would probably reply **C**.

Play forcing moves when you have to, then abandon them.

This proverb is related to another saying in this book, "Don't try to save worthless stones," and generally applies to making a light, flexible shape in your opponent's sphere of influence. The idea is to first make moves in the area that must be answered, usually to leave you good aji for eye shape or later forcing moves. The next step is to either escape or make a base, leaving the forcing moves to fend for themselves until needed.

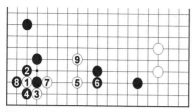

Figure 53. Force, extend, then run away.

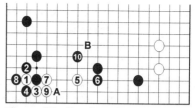

Figure 54. Don't make the group heavy.

Figure 53. White 1 strikes at the heart of the double wing formation and black has a number or ways to respond. If black chooses to protect his corner with 2 and 4, white plays on the outside with 5, which aims at the thinness of the two black stones to the right. Black will probably defend with 6, so white forces once more with 7 then jumps with 9.

Figure 54. This figure shows what happens when you go against this proverb. If white connects with 9 or **A**, black caps with 10 and white is in real trouble.

Note that there is no reason to play 9 – black won't bother capturing white 3 until the end game (it is worth about two points in gote, since white ataris with **A**). At this point in the game, white should have jumped to 10 then, if black captures 3, white would stick his head out even farther with **B**.

A severe invasion on the third line or a gentle one on the fourth?

Unfortunately, there is no reliable rule of thumb to guide you in choosing between the third and fourth lines when invading an enemy position on the side. It is a matter of the surrounding position. There are times when one is better than the other, and when one may be very bad.

Reading is the key, of course, and you have to consider the peculiarities of each position before invading. If you have examined all the possibilities carefully, choose the invasion that is more painful to your opponent and less threatening to your surrounding positions.

In general, the third-line invasion is relatively weak in escaping toward the center to escape, whereas the fourth-line play has the advantage of speed if the opponent seems likely to start a running fight. On the other hand, if the invader can live and the blockade is not worth much, a play on the third line is the better choice.

Chapter 10
A Guide to Fighting

Take territory while attacking.

You've probably heard the proverbs warning against trying to surround the center directly and against playing near thickness, and wondered just how you're supposed to get compensation for the points you've given your opponent while building up center influence.

The answer is: Attack! Your stones are strong, with few weak points, and you want to drive the enemy forces into your strong positions.

The idea is to accumulate territory while you attack. Your opponent's group is under considerable pressure to survive and has few options; the moves he is making are working at perhaps 50% efficiency. You, on the other hand, are free to direct the fight pretty much as you want and can make 100% effective moves.

This is why moyos are supposed to be reduced gently with a shoulder hit or capping play unless there are weak points that you can aim at to invade successfully. Letting the other player direct local operations is a considerable disadvantage.

If your opponent happens to make a reducing move, you have no reason to be dissatisfied, though. If counterattacking would be an overplay, you just take territory. If your defense is ignored, sooner or later the reducing move will become an attractive target.

When you read out a fight in which you have the option to build influence, try to visualize your resulting thickness, any invasions and reducing moves, and their counters. In some cases, a rough estimate of your gain on the outside will help guide you to how much territory you should cede to the other side in building your wall. Just remember that such estimates are rough and don't rely too heavily on them. Go is more complicated than that.

A word of warning – Don't make the mistake of thinking that the whole moyo is yours. It isn't. If you have played correctly, you should realize about as many points as you gave your opponent when you made the wall, and you can be happy with that. There is real danger in going into a feeding frenzy and going all out to kill something you should just chase.

Defend while attacking.
Attack while defending.

Perhaps the most profitable skill in go is the ability to combine both offense and defense in the same move. This is one of the skills that characterize the play of dan players.

Try to be constantly aware of the weak points in both your opponent's and your own positions, and search for moves that protect your group's defects and expose those of the other side at the same time. It is very satisfying to play a move that enlarges your territory or protects a cutting point while setting up an invasion that will devastate your opponent unless he answers.

Don't give up key stones.

This proverb indicates the importance of cutting stones. If you have killed a group or have a very strong attack on it, the stones that cut it off or prevent it from getting life become vital and you must protect them.

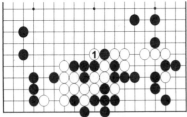

Figure 1. What should black do?

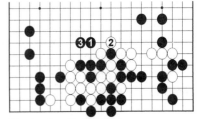

Figure 2. Shortsighted.

Figure 1. White has just played atari with 1. Considering the overall position, how should black answer?

Figure 2. White is counting on black's emotional attachment to the four stones. Unfortunately, white 2 connects to the endangered stones on the right, and white has no worries.

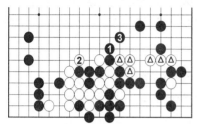

Figure 3. The correct answer.

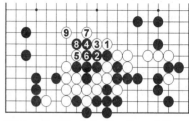

Figure 4. Much better for white.

Figure 3. According to the proverb, black should simply extend with 1. If white follows through with 2, then black 3 grabs nearly thirty points when the escape route of the marked white stones is cut off.

Figure 4. Actually, white ataried from the wrong side. There is no reason to go after the four stones, since the white group at the bottom is alive. If black resists with 2 instead of allowing the connection and jumping to 4 right away, something like this follows and black has lost quite a bit.

Don't weaken your own stones.

There is a tendency among weaker players to take profit while weakening their own nearby stones; such petty greed only helps the opponent win the game.

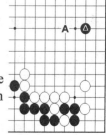

Figure 5. Don't weaken your own stones!

Figure 5. Black played the marked stone too close to the white wall, so white jumped in at 1 hoping that black would automatically attach and make white stronger here. This is a bad exchange for black. Granted, the marked stone is unlikely to die, but at this point it looks as though black has invaded deeply into a white moyo and nothing good can come of it.

Black should have jumped out to **A** instead of strengthening white's stone. Then white would have had to do something about 1 (perhaps an attachment of his own or a 3–3 invasion), and black could have jumped again, very nicely reducing the effect of the white wall.

Don't make two weak groups. Beware the splitting attack.

Having one weak group on the board is unfortunate. Having two is quite bad, especially if there is a strong enemy position between them, which invites a splitting attack.

The splitting attack is extremely effective because the strong group in the middle can jump out and threaten two groups at once. It is worth an extra move to strengthen one of the groups to prevent such an assault.

This is one of the dangers of the type of go where players like to "mix it up" and get many insecure groups running after each other at once. It is very easy to make one of the groups strong enough to start a splitting attack that will catch one group or the other.

Master the splitting and leaning attacks.

The splitting and leaning attacks become useful when there are two weak enemy groups in the same general area of the board, and are often used in combination.

The splitting attack consists of a series of moves from a strong position out between two enemy groups. This efficient technique allows you to attack both groups with each move, while your opponent needs a move to strengthen each group and will quickly fall behind. Obviously, at some point, one or both groups will be at a real disadvantage.

The leaning attack is used when the two groups are more widely separated. In this case, you play directly against the stones that you are *less* interested in so that you can build thickness against which you will drive the stones that you really want to attack.

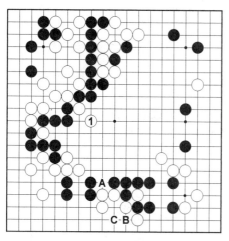

Figure 6. In this position from a professional game, white starts a splitting attack by pulling out the single stone with 1. The black group at the top has no eyes and the one at the left has only one, so this is ideal. Also, white can push through at **A**. (Black **B** then white **C** lets white's group at the bottom live with ko.)

Figure 6. Kobayashi (W) v Kato: beginning the splitting attack.

Figure 7. Black defends with 2 through 14 to make sure that his two groups are alive. White, for his part, has built considerable thickness in the center and this is adequate compensation for the attack.

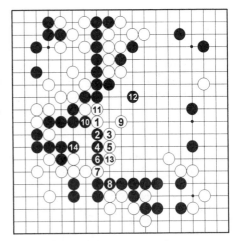

Figure 7. Black plays to make sure his two groups are alive.

Figure 8. White continues with 1 to start a leaning attack. Of course, he is looking at the black group at the top when he does this.

If black answers at **A**, the pressure continues with **B**, **C**, and **D**, and black's group at the top is in desperate straits.

Black answers as shown but he still has problems.

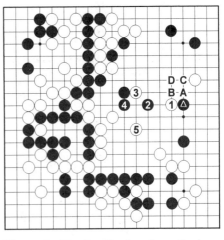

Figure 8. Starting the leaning attack.

Don't touch stones you want to attack.

Playing directly against a stone is a severe move that usually elicits a response, making the opponent's stone much stronger. This is the last thing you want to do to stones that you want to attack, so you have to learn to attack from a distance and encircle the enemy on a large scale.

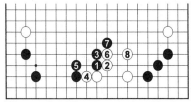

Figure 9. Wrong way to attack.   Figure 10. Attack at a distance.

Figure 9. Black has attached to one of white's stones, forcing the sequence shown here. White now has a solid, living shape and black has defeated his own purpose.

Figure 10. It's far better to attack from a distance – the capping move is one of the best methods for harassing this two-stone group. After this, black will attach at **A** to start a leaning attack by trying to make a wall to run the attacked group into. (Black's not interested in attacking the single white stone right now, so he can play directly against it.)

Don't let your stones get squeezed flat.

The usefulness of your opponent's sacrifice stones can sometimes be reduced by squeezing them flat with a series of forcing moves. On the other hand, if you can capture some stones, try to find a way to introduce defects in the enemy position when you take them and avoid having your own stones squeezed flat.

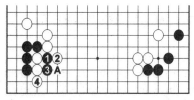

Figure 11. Add another sacrifice stone.

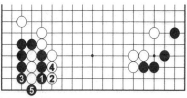

Figure 12. Now white gets a perfect wall.

Figure 11. From black's point of view, there is no way that the cut of 1 can fail to turn out well – white can't play 2 at 3 and chase black into the strong moyo (this is a sure way to lose, and black's left corner is alive in any case), so black can expect to capture a couple of stones at the very least. White adds one more stone to the sacrifice with 4 (playing at **A** is out of the question). So far, this is a standard sequence.

Figure 12. Black wants to capture the stones as quickly as possible, but white is happy to force with 2 and 4, build a perfect wall in the center with sente, and move on to a big point somewhere else.

Figure 13. Black 1 is the move to make things right – it still captures the three white stones but nudges out into the white moyo a bit and allows black to keep sente since white has to protect the cut at A. Compare this

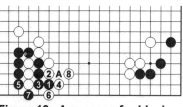

Figure 13. A success for black.

result to that in the last figure and you'll find quite a difference.

Moves 1 through 8 are forced, but consider white 8 for a moment – white can't really avoid playing there. Weak players often ignore the need to protect against such cuts but later, when their opponent starts a fight to reduce the moyo, find themselves fighting twice as hard trying to cover this defect.

Attack after making the other stones heavy.

Stones can be said to be heavy or light. A group is said to be heavy, or overconcentrated, if it uses more stones than needed and will have trouble making eyes. On the other hand, a group is said to be light if its stones have an airy, flexible shape and the potential for making eyes (or escape) easily. If necessary, light stones can be given up with little loss if they have forced the opponent to reply.

Heavy stones are a burden on their owner – they can't make eyes very well, so they often have to scurry out to the center where they are a welcome target. Because they lack a flexible shape, it is relatively easy for the opponent to aim at vital points and, if they die, the owner usually loses a lot of points.

This proverb tells you to first make your opponent's stones heavy before starting the real attack. You can do this with a peep (as shown below), by threatening to cut, or even by attaching in some cases.

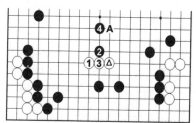

Figure 14. Peep to make the invader heavy.

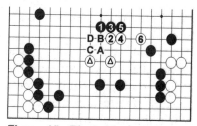

Figure 15. Black 1 is a slack move.

Figure 14. The marked white stone went a little too deeply into black's moyo but the real mistake was in playing 1 instead of jumping lightly to **A**. Black responds immediately, threatening to cut the two stones and surround about thirty points on the left side while chasing the fleeing group.

Figure 15 (last page). Putting aside the peep for the moment, black prevents white from taking the point of 1 and making the excellent shape known as the horse's face. Unfortunately, white simply continues as shown to escape. Now, when black tries to peep (**A** in this figure), white simply continues with **B** and gives up the two stones, squeezing black as he goes.

Don't make only one huge territory.

It's often said "Don't put all your eggs in one basket," and the same applies to go. This proverb points out the danger of "moyo overkill" – trying to surround a huge area without a few other groups on the board to contribute to your territory. There's absolutely nothing wrong with playing a moyo strategy, but too much of a good thing is bad for your game!

There are good reasons for this warning. First, building an overblown moyo usually gives the opponent a lot of solid territory, possibly on the fourth or even fifth line. Knowing that the moyo has to yield at least, say, eighty points can be a real burden psychologically.

There is also the difficulty in sealing off all four sides of a large moyo. At any point, the opponent can play a reducing move that will erase a large part of it, probably increasing his own prospects at the same time (instead of retreating, the defender might consider starting an unreasonable fight, which will erode the moyo further if it doesn't work).

Finally, there is almost always an invasion somewhere if all else fails. Even a small life can destroy a third of the moyo's potential. Building huge frameworks and hoping that your opponent will make a mistake is no way to play go.

Don't try to surround an area with an open skirt.

An "open skirt" occurs when a position is open at the side so that the opponent can slide into the area with a keima or a one-point jump. This weakness makes it much less profitable to try to make the position into actual territory. The problem is that, when you try to close off one side, the opponent comes in the other (or reduces from the other direction as the case may be).

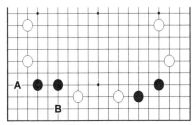

Figure 16. The left corner is open at A and B.

Figure 17. White slides with 2.

Figure 16. The black position on the left has two open skirts – white can slide in at **A** or **B**. It's black's turn: where should he play?

Figure 17. Black 1 here is, of course, not an option. White simply slides in at 2 and, whatever happens, black's corner is going to be very small. Black should have closed off the other corner at the 2–4 or 3–4 point.

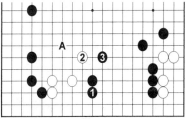

Figure 18. Taking territory while attacking.

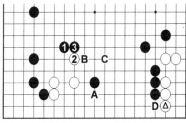

Figure 19. An open skirt changes everything.

Figure 18 (last page). This figure is given to show how drastically an open skirt can affect nearby fighting. Black has a fine moyo and the white stones don't have clear eye shape yet, so he begins the attack with the "iron pillar" of 1. White has to run out into the center, and 2 is as good as anything. Black 3 continues the attack, surrounding about twenty points in a single gulp.

Figure 19 (last page). Now suppose that white had played the marked stone at some point. Because black's moyo has an open skirt, closing it off has become quite secondary and black begins the attack this time with 1, since the iron pillar is not so effective any more. White runs with 2, then black builds some real thickness at the top with 3.

If black had followed the sequence of the last diagram here (black **A**, white **B**, black **C**), white's group would be in the clear and black would be open to the turn of **D** or the one-point jump to the left of it. This is not playable for black when there is an open skirt at the right.

Figure 20. There are a number of big points to choose from. Where should white play? (Consider where black would like to play if it were his turn – this is a handy rule of thumb.)

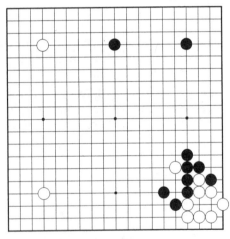

Figure 20. White to play.

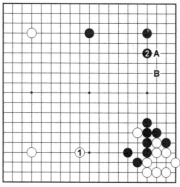
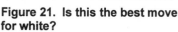

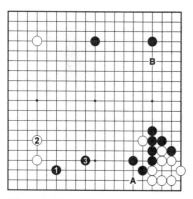

Figure 21. Is this the best move for white?

Figure 22. If it were his move, would black play here?

Figure 21. Considering all the thickness that black has built on the right side, playing white 1 to reduce its value is natural, but this is a purely local move. Black just makes the one-point jump at 2 and his moyo is looking serious indeed – this is a huge move.

White 1 has to be at **A** in the figure to break up black's moyo into more manageable pieces. After this, black will probably answer at **B**, staying as far from his wall as possible.

Figure 22. If you imagined black playing 1 in this diagram, you missed the open skirt at **A**, which makes the lower side uninteresting for the time being. That is why both sides want to play in the upper right corner, a first-class move in every respect. The lower side is a second- or third-class area because of the open skirt.

The weak player pushes without thinking.

Weak players like to play forcing moves just to keep sente. You often see them pushing their opponents' stones along regardless of the consequences. Sometimes they are afraid that the other side will attack their stones, other times they are just imitating a strong player in an inappropriate situation. More often than not, these forcing moves do more harm than good.

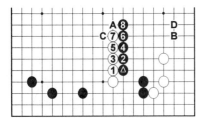

Figure 23. This only strengthens the weak black stones.

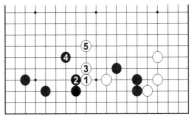

Figure 24. The correct answer: the black stones are weaker.

Figure 23. Black has just played the shoulder hit with the marked stone, so white has to do something to prevent his stone from being swallowed up. In this case, white has panicked and pushed up, step by step strengthening the black stones (**A** will be a good point for black later).

The white wall has very little effect on the black position to the left but, backed by the new black wall, the approach at **B** now hits white's right-corner position where it hurts. Clearly, this exchange has been very bad for white. Even if white had to push this way, he should have jumped ahead with the knight's move at **C** instead of 5, which would have allowed white to answer 6 with **D** and patch things up somewhat.

Figure 24. The best answer is for white to start a leaning attack by making a shoulder hit of his own. After white 3 and 5, black's three stones are looking rather weak. This is a tremendous difference from the position in the last diagram.

Never push on the fifth or sixth lines.

The fourth line is said the be the line of victory because each move gains three points of territory. Avoid at all costs pushing your opponent along the line of victory – it's tough to be sure that you'll realize three points for every stone in your wall. It follows that you don't want to help your opponent by pushing on the fifth line, which is even worse.

Figure 25. White jumps with 1 to get into the center, but instead of playing at 9 next to follow joseki, he keeps pushing along the fifth line, perhaps thinking that this will make the attack on the marked black stone more severe.

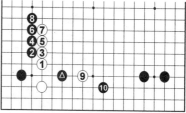

Figure 25. Don't push on the fifth line.

Black is happy to continue grabbing territory. When white finally plays 9, black makes a counter-pincer with 10 and the white stones are very overconcentrated. White has given his opponent more than fifteen points by pushing him along – how can he ever make that up?

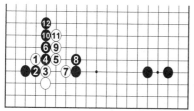

Figure 26. Pushing on the sixth line is even worse.

Figure 27. The correct joseki.

Figure 26. This is a different joseki but the same idea, except this time white is pushing on the sixth line and forcing black to take four points of territory with each push. This is forcing your opponent to win the game.

Figure 27. This is the correct way to play. If black plays 6 at **A**, for example, white 5 threatens the sequence white 6, black **B**, 7, etc. and black is at a disadvantage. Therefore, black extends with 6 and the joseki continues as shown.

Chapter 11
A Potpourri of Proverbs

The monkey jump is worth eight points.

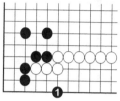

Figure 1. A monkey jump.

Figure 2. The correct counter here.

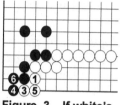

Figure 3. If white's turn. . . .

Figure 1. The large knight's move on the first line shown here is known as a "monkey jump." (Sliding in only as far as a knight's move gives us the small monkey jump.) The monkey jump is said to be worth eight points, but this depends on the local position, and there are many variations.

Figure 2. White 1 is the correct response here, although playing at 2 or **A** may be correct under other circumstances. Later white can play **B** forcing **C**, then atari at **A**.

Figure 3. If white blocks at 1, then 3 through 6 are his privilege. The differences in the black and white territories between this diagram and the last is eight points.

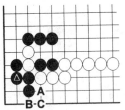

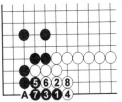

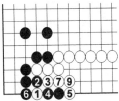

Figure 4. A monkey jump is worth six points here.

Figure 5. This white 2 loses a point.

Figure 6. This white 1 also loses a point. (8@1)

Figure 4. This figure shows a slightly different position. Now if white blocks at **A**, the hane of **B** is no longer sente because of the marked black stone. This makes the monkey jump worth only six points.

Figures 5 and 6. These white moves are often seen but, in this position, they lose one point (black gets the extra territory at **A** in one figure and a prisoner in the other).

The first-line hane and connection is worth two points.

The next two figures show a common end-game position. The hane and connection here is worth two points in gote although, in other positions, it can be worth three or four points.

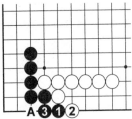

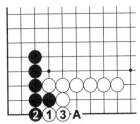

Figure 7. Black gains one point by playing first.

Figure 8. White gains one point by playing first.

Figures 7 and 8. Whoever moves first gains the point of territory marked **A**. The difference in local score between the two figures is a total of two points.

The second-line hane and connection is worth six points.

Another common end-game combination is the hane and connection on the second line, worth six points to whoever takes it first. Again, there are exceptions depending on nearby stones – in other positions, the combination is worth eight to fourteen points.

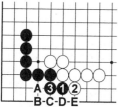

Figure 9. Black gets three points by playing first.

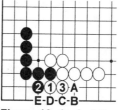

Figure 10. And white gets three points by playing first.

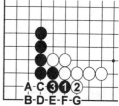

Figure 11. In this example, playing first is worth five points for black.

Figures 9 and 10. Whoever moves first gains the three points of territory marked **A**, **B**, and **C**. Because, at this point in the game, we have no idea of who will play the first-line hane of **E** and connection, we simplify the counting by assuming an average, that each player descends immediately to **D** or **E**. The difference in local score between the two figures is a total of six points.

Figure 11. Here is a position in which the end-game combination is worth eight points. Because the eventual white hane on the first line will be worth two points in sente (Figure 12), black gains the points marked **A** through **E** as territory by playing first.

Figure 12. White gains three points by playing first here, plus he has the sente sequence of **D**, **E**, **F**, and **G** mentioned above. The difference between Figures 11 and 12 is eight points.

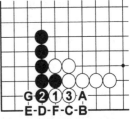

Figure 12. White gains three points by playing first.

Look for the best move even when losing.

There is a tendency for some people, when they have just lost a small group or discover themselves to be at a positional disadvantage, to change their style of play for the worse.

You should always try to find the best move on the board, regardless of whether you are ahead or behind. If you can't do this, you might as well resign, otherwise the game won't be interesting for either of you.

Actually, finding yourself at an initial disadvantage is a great opportunity to learn and improve. Your opponent may well start playing slack moves that you can turn to your advantage in the middle game, and it's not unheard of to pick up an extra ten points or more in the end game.

You are two stones stronger when watching a game.

Have you ever watched someone who gives you a tough time in an even game and noticed all the silly mistakes they make when playing someone else? You have to wonder why they don't do you the same favor when they are playing with you.

The truth is, they probably do. Maybe not the same mistakes, but misreadings and errors in judgement of the same order. You just don't have the same emotional involvement in the game when you are watching and can be more objective about what is really happening on the board.

One of the best, but perhaps hardest, ways to become stronger is to strive for a calm, detached attitude when you play go. This can add a stone, or maybe two, to your strength if you are an emotional player. It is easy to become attached to stones that might better be sacrificed or left alone for the moment. If the opponent makes an overplay, it's hard to wait to punish it when the situation calls for you to strengthen something else before starting the offensive.

One technique that may help is to mentally "disconnect" from the game as often as you can, then come back and look at the board position as though it were a problem in a book. Determine anew which groups are strong, which are weak, where the aji is that has to be watched, what the balance of territory is, how much thickness is worth, and so forth.

There is no defeat in go.

This proverb says several things. First, playing go is an experience that enriches your life. It also tells you not to brood over your losses and to be humble about your victories.

For a few, go is just a way to pass a couple of hours while they have nothing better to do. But for many, go helps to improve memory and analytical skills, to develop their sense of balance, and to make friends all over the world (thanks to the availability of internet go servers [try telnet igs.joyjoy.net 6969 and nngs.cosmic.org 9696, and don't forget the rec.games.go newsgroup]).

Even when you lose a game, you win in a sense. Keep a record of your games and, after a day or two so to restore objectivity, study them. Try to find a stronger player who is willing to go over them with you. You can learn a lot from your mistakes, and you'll improve very quickly.

And remember, over time you will win as many games as you lose. So don't fret over games you should have won and keep your eye on the big picture – your goal should be to improve as quickly as you can.

Killing stones won't win the game.
Losing stones won't lose the game.

These proverbs say that you shouldn't allow the capture of a few stones to affect your game. The fate of a meaningless group doesn't really matter, but you will see players willing to do everything they can to rescue a couple of stones under heavy attack. These players allow the fight to spill over into their own moyo or give the opponent overwhelming outside influence, huge losses even if they do eke out a small life.

If you find a small group coming under attack, ask yourself whether the stones have an easy escape route. Will their escape weaken your nearby positions? Can you make useful moves on the outside to force the capture of the stones?

If you can escape easily without hurting your other positions, do so lightly and be ready to give up the first stones to come under attack. You don't want to connect and make a large heavy group that you can't afford to lose. (There is a matter of scale to consider in applying this proverb: losing a couple of dozen stones will almost certainly cost you the game.)

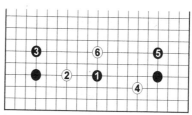

Figure 13. A standard position from handicap go.

Figure 13. Here's a position that is quite common in handicap go, usually found in games of four stones and up. White's cap of 6 is frightening, but it is actually quite loose and black should be able to escape easily (the article "Don't make empty triangles" shows one way). White has a number of options to complicate the way out, though, so in large handicap games black might consider making white capture the stone on a small scale.

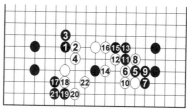

Figure 14. Make white capture on a small scale.

Figure 14. After white captures the single stone, black has amassed nearly fifty points of territory, compared to white's twenty-odd points. This is a great trade, if black can manage it; but if white plays so passively, he probably shouldn't be giving a handicap.

Still, this does show how effective giving up a stone can be instead of trying to run away with it and giving your opponent a heavy group to attack.

Don't play bizarre moves.

There is a class of go players who have to kill everything and will do anything to win. They include in their repertoire overplays, trick moves, and the truly bizarre. Go clubs abound with these bullies. Don't be one of them.

Ask yourself why you play go. Of course it's a pleasant way to pass the time, but most people enjoy the mental exercise and take great satisfaction from growing stronger at the game as well. Several professionals have said "The day I stop learning something new is the day I quit go."

Playing dishonest moves alters your perception of the game and your "go instincts"– and makes it much harder to make progress. It's far better in the long run to lose a few games and learn the correct way to deal with troublesome situations than hoping that the opponent won't come up with the proper counter.

In short, play the honest move, learn trick moves so you can refute them, and go over your games carefully to see how you could have played better.

If you lose four corners, resign.

This may be the most famous go proverb of all. Letting the other person get four corners' worth of territory is often enough to win the game, especially if he has points in other parts of the board.

Takemiya Masaki, 9p, is the exception to the rule with his thickness-oriented "cosmic" style of go. Here is one of his games:

Figure 15. In this professional game, Takemiya took white and gave up four corners to build up outside influence. He went on to win the game by half a point.

By the way, after Takemiya started winning consistently with this strategy, some people started saying "If you take four corners, resign," but this is not sound advice for any but the very best.

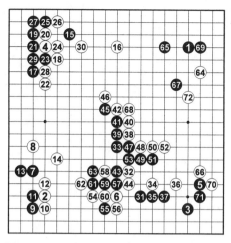

Figure 15. The "cosmic" go of Takemiya.

Glossary

This glossary defines technical terms and phrases used in this book that may be unfamiliar to the average reader. Most of them have been retained from the Japanese original because they are shorter than their English equivalents or because there is no easy translation.

The key to pronunciations given after Japanese terms is as follows: *ä* as in **father**; *ā* as in **make**; *ai* as in **aisle**; *ĕ* as in **egg**; *ē* almost as in **even**; *ō* as in **open**; and *ŭ* as in **look**.

aji (ä-jē)

The tactical potential of a position that is not immediately utilized. Aji is said to be good or bad.

atari (ä-tä-rē)

Check, as in chess, which warns that a stone or group will be surrounded and removed from the board on the next move if nothing is done. Also, the state of being in atari. It is customary to warn of an atari when you make one.

attachment

A move that is played against an enemy stone.

bottle shape

A knight's move from two stones separated by one space. Can form bad shape, but not always. Also called the dog's face.

cap, capping move

A move two points above an enemy stone.

dame (dä-mě)

A liberty, or a neutral point.

dan (dän)

A rank given to strong players. Amateurs are ranked from one dan to seven dan (1d – 7d), with a one-stone difference between ranks. Professional are ranked from one dan to nine dan (1p – 9p), with a one-third stone difference per rank. Professional one dan is roughly equivalent to amateur seven dan.

dog's face

A knight's move from two stones separated by one space. Can form bad shape, but not always. Also called the bottle shape.

empty triangle

One of the classic bad shapes.

eye

An independent internal liberty. A group needs two eyes to live.

giraffe's neck

A move that is one space farther than the horse's face from two stones that are separated by one space.

gote (gō-tě)

A move that doesn't have to be answered at the moment. A move may be gote at one point in the game but sente later on.

gote no sente (gō-tĕ nō sĕn-tĕ)

A move that doesn't have to be answered at the moment but has a follow up that is sente.

hane (hä-nĕ)

A diagonal move from a stone that "wraps around" an enemy stone.

heavy

Refers to stones that are clumped together or otherwise don't have good shape (eye-making potential, an abundance of good follow-up moves, etc.).

horse's face

A large-knight's move from two stones that are separated by one space.

hoshi (hō-shē)

One of the nine star points on the board.

iron pillar

A move on the third line, dropping down directly from a side star point. A specialty move, good only in certain situations.

joseki (jō-sĕ-kē)

A corner pattern that is locally equal for both sides. However, a given joseki can be totally inappropriate to the whole-board situation and thus entail considerable loss.

keima (kā-mă)

A knight's move.

ko (kō)

Refers to a local situation in which, the players could capture and recapture a stone, theoretically forever. To prevent this infinite waste of time, one of the rules of the game states that, after a player takes a ko, the other must play elsewhere before retaking it.

komi (kō-mē)

The number of points given white to compensate for black's advantage of having the first move. Also the system awarding such compensation (old games were played without komi, that is, black only had to win on the board).

kosumi (kō-sŭ-mē)

A diagonal move from a friendly stone.

ko threat

A forcing move played so that a player can retake a ko.

kyu

The rank given players who have not reached dan strength. Absolute beginners are about thirty kyu (30k). It can take a player anywhere from one to five years to leave the kyu ranks and become a dan player.

light

Refers to stones that are well-positioned and have good shape (eye-making potential, an abundance of good follow-up moves, etc.).

miai (mē-ai)

Literally, "seeing together." Refers to two points such that, if one player takes one, the other player can handle the situation by taking the other point.

moyo (mō-yō)

A large framework of potential territory.

nakade (nä-kä-dě)

A play made in an eye space to reduce it to a single eye. The shape made by such a play.

ogeima (ō-gä-mă)

A large-knight's move.

ponnuki (pän-nŭ-kē)

The shape made with four stones after they have captured a stone. A very desirable shape.

sanrensei (sän-rěn-sā)

The position or opening in which one player occupies all three star points on one side of the board.

seki (sě-kē)

A position in which two groups, neither with two eyes, are both alive because of a shortage of liberties.

semeai (sě-mě-ai)

A race to capture between two groups.

sente (sĕn-tĕ)

A move that has to be answered at the moment. A move may be sente at one point in the game but gote later on.

shimari (shē-mä-rē)

A corner enclosure, usually of two stones.

soldier's helmet

One of the classic bad shapes.

tesuji (tĕ-sŭ-jē)

A tactically strong move in the local position.

thick

Said of stones that have few, if any, weaknesses; such stones usually face the center or side and exert influence over the nearby area.

yose (yō-sĕ)

The end game of go.

INDEX

Books From Yutopian

Sakata Series
Killer of Go
Tesuji and Anti-Suji of Go

The Nihon Ki-In Series
A Compendium of Trick Plays
100 Challenging Go Problems for 100 Days of Study
Pro-Pro Handicap Go

Go Handbook Series
Go Proverbs
Fuseki   (available 1999)

Chinese Professional Series
Nie WeiPing on Go
Thirty-Six Stratagems Applied to Go, by Ma XiaoChun
Beauty and the Beast, Exquisite Play and Go Theory by Shen Guosun
Golden Opportunities by Rin Kaiho
Winning A Won Game, by Go Seigen
Yang Yilun's Ingenious Life and Death Puzzles, vol. 1 and 2
Essential Joseki by Rui Naiwei
Power Builder, vol. 1, by Wang Runan
Strategic Fundamentals in Go, by Guo Tisheng   (available 1999)

Art of Go Series
Art of Connecting Stones
Art of Capturing   (available 1999)

Pocket Book Series, by Yang Yilun
Rescue and Capture
Tricks in Joseki   (available 1999)

Korean Series
Cho HunHyun's Go Techniques, vol. 1
Lee ChangHo's Novel Plays and Shapes   (available 1999)

Other Books From Yutopian
Fighting Ko
Utilizing Outward Influence
Master Go in Ten Days
Dramatic Moments on the Go Board
Igo Hatsuyo-ron, vol. 1